COOKING FOR
CHAPS

Gustav Temple has been editor of The Chap since 1999 and
is the author of four books. Gustav is an expert on matters of
social and sartorial etiquette and has appeared on numerous
mainstream television and radio channels.

Clare Gabbett-Mulhallen has cooked professionally for 20
years. She took a Diploma in Cordon Bleu at Tante Marie and
later worked as a cook in grand private houses, at Eton College
and at Bucks Club. She won a Great Taste Award in 2007.

COOKING FOR CHAPS

STYLISH, NO-NONSENSE MEALS FOR THE MAN ABOUT TOWN

Gustav Temple and
Clare Gabbett-Mulhallen

Photography by Sophie Broadbridge

Kyle Books

To Theo and Romilly.
— *Gustav*

For the little chaps: my son Dax, my nephew Ethan, my niece Greta
and my Godson Oscar.
And Patroclas, magnificent at liberty.
— *Clare*

....

First published in Great Britain in 2014 by
Kyle Books, an imprint of Kyle Cathie Ltd
192–198 Vauxhall Bridge Road
London SW1V 1DX
general.enquiries@kylebooks.com
www.kylebooks.com

Printer line 10 9 8 7 6 5 4 3 2 1

ISBN 978 0 85783 225 2

Text © 2014 Gustav Temple and Clare Gabbett-Mulhallen
Design © 2014 Kyle Books
Photographs © 2014 Sophie Broadbridge
Illustrations © 2014 David Hitch

Project Editor: Tara O'Sullivan
Copy Editor: Stephanie Evans
Designer: Katie Moorman
Photographer: Sophie Broadbridge
Illustrator: David Hitch
Food Stylist: Rosie Reynolds
Prop Stylists: Wei Tang and Sarah Waller
Production: Nic Jones and Gemma John

A Cataloguing in Publication record for this title is available from the British Library.

Colour reproduction by ALTA London
Printed and bound in Singapore by Tien Wah Press

CONTENTS

A chap's approach to cooking is as traditional, practical, thorough and sensible – with a little dash of the decadent – as everything else in his life.

INTRODUCTION

How can a chap, most of whose time is spent twirling his moustachios and selecting which of his silver-topped Malacca canes to take to the opera, find any time to do any cooking? You could be forgiven for asking this question, but the truth is that cooking is, in fact, a most chappish pursuit. One might have expected a chap's dining habits to be limited to lunch at his club or being cooked lavish suppers at home by a fleet of servants. But there is more to him than that: for a chap likes to do everything *properly*. Whether this means wearing the correct type of Marcella bow tie with evening dress or making a perfectly pitched witty remark to a Madagascan prince, a chap will always adhere to the rule book in his mind, in which are listed all the appropriate colours, fabrics, positions and utterances that he considers it proper to adopt for each given circumstance. And when it comes to cookery, he is equally precise. A chap is far more likely to be able to rustle up a single obscure dish such as Beef Wellington than he is to be seen distressing a bowl of the latest faddish salad vegetable with yet another new type of olive oil.

A chap's approach to cooking is as traditional, practical, thorough and sensible – with a little dash of the decadent – as is everything else in his life. He looks to the recipes his forefathers used; if he is lucky, he may even have a few of them, handwritten by some long-deceased retainer of his great uncle. He does not approve of contemporary cookbooks because the celebrity chef does not entice him (not owning a television, he doesn't know who they are anyway). He may own the classics – Elizabeth David, Constance Spry, Rosemary Hume – and he also owns a few first editions of fairly obscure though well-thought-of-at-the-time cookery writers, such as Colonel Kenney-Herbert.

Colonel Kenney-Herbert, a cavalry officer serving under the British Raj in India, was one of the few who sallied forth into the kitchens of Calcutta to find out what was going on. He was so disgusted with the conditions and the supplies that he immediately set about making improvements and laid out his forceful opinions on English and Indian cookery in several cookbooks, notably *Culinary Jottings* (1878). When he returned to England in the 1920s, his disdain for the state of contemporary cookery came with him. He founded the Commonsense Cookery Association, which advocated simple, thorough cooking without waste and over ornamentation: 'Finikin decoration – the making of "pretty-pretty" dishes at the cost of flavour and much valuable time – is a mistake in private houses where the kitchen staff consists of two or three persons.' You could easily say the same thing to many a celebrity restaurateur.

Several of Colonel Kenney-Herbert's books dealt specifically with Indian cuisine, with which in Britain we are all now extremely familiar. But we should like to know what happened to the recipes contained in the same author's *Fifty Breakfasts* (1894). How did we end up with a typical English breakfast menu in a café that is essentially twelve versions of the same meal? The Colonel didn't just offer gastronomic advice; he also had strong opinions on etiquette, delivered in his stentorian military tones: 'You sometimes see a hungry man polish off his bivalves before the lime, pepper and bread and butter have reached him. You can combat this contingency by breaking up the dishes containing these adjuncts into detachments, and serving them in two or three directions at once.'

As well as looking to the great cooks of the past for inspiration, we consulted the great fictional gourmands too: Harry Palmer, James Bond, Bertie Wooster. The characters' love of fine dining reflected that of their authors. Len Deighton, creator of Harry

Palmer, even wrote his own cookbook, *Len Deighton's Action Cook Book*. This was long before the dawn of the male celebrity chef with his macho approach to the pestle and mortar, and the very title of Leighton's book sounded like an apology for being a cookbook aimed at men. We have included one of Deighton's omelettes in this book, the one that Harry Palmer (Michael Caine) cooks for Courtney (Sue Lloyd) in *The Ipcress File*. 'That was the most delicious meal,' says Courtney afterwards. 'Tell me, do you always wear those glasses?'. 'Always,' says Harry, 'except in bed.' Courtney reaches for the spectacles.

James Bond was another fictional gourmet heavily influenced by his creator's tastes. As well as sharing Fleming's golf handicap (9) and his shampoo (Pinaud Elixir), Bond shares his creator's taste for upper class dining staples from around the world (though he is not averse to enjoying a bit of rustic fare, as he does in the form of a Mutton Ragout at a gypsy camp outside Istanbul in *From Russia With Love*). A typical Bond breakfast would consist of two large cups of very strong coffee from De Bry in New Oxford Street, a French Maran egg boiled for three-and-a-third minutes, wholewheat toast, Jersey butter and a choice of Tiptree 'Little Scarlet' strawberry jam, Cooper's Vintage Oxford marmalade and Norwegian Heather Honey from Fortnum and Mason. There was no time for all this in the film versions and Bond's fussy dining habits only get a cursory mention – in the remake of *Casino Royale*, Daniel Craig's Bond is even seen drinking vodka martinis with dinner, at which Fleming would have been horrified.

In the book version of *Goldfinger*, Bond enjoys such a vast succession of sumptuous meals in pursuit of Auric Goldfinger that it is surprising he ever catches up with his quarry, and even more surprising that he is able to throw a single punch, weighed down as he is with cheese soufflé, curried shrimps, *sole meunière*, roast duck, *quenelles de brochet*, *gratin de langoustes* and rib of beef in red wine. *Cooking for Chaps* aims to be more faithful to the Fleming version of James Bond.

Bertie Wooster could never be accused of gluttony and the contents of the dinner table only receive a passing mention in the Jeeves books, until the arrival of Anatole in *The Code of the Woosters*. Aunt Dahlia's admired and sought-after French chef has made Bertie's favourite dish, Timbale de Riz de Veau Toulousaine, but there is the threat of him being farmed out to one of Dahlia's cousins.

'It's difficult to convey to those who have not tasted this wizard's products the extraordinary importance which his roasts and boileds assume in the scheme of things to those who have. I can only say that once having bitten into one of his dishes you are left with the feeling that life will be deprived of all its poetry and meaning unless you are in a position to go on digging in.'

These days, Anatole would have his own television show and chaps are expected to pull their weight in the kitchen. Gone are the slick-haired Jeeveses shimmering about the place, their fish-filled brains instinctively anticipating the precise snack, repast or hangover cure required by their employer. Chaps have to fend for themselves and anticipate their own needs and those of their house guests, though we have included a couple of meals specifically designed to chivvy along unwanted guests. We may have lost our Jeeveses, but ravenous maiden aunts continue to plague our households. Our High Tea chapter suggests the dexterous serving of a table groaning with gastronomic delights; the rationing of cutlery to one fork each ensures that the guests do not hang around all evening.

Dinner parties, according to Nigel Slater, are only given by antique dealers and homosexuals, but this is no reason not to invite a few chums over for supper,

> Gone are the slick-haired Jeeveses shimmering about the place, their fish-filled brains instinctively anticipating the precise snack, repast or hangover cure required by their employer. ✔

whatever their professions and sexual proclivities. We are all for lavish entertaining, but too many television cookery programmes seem to counsel turning one's home into an ersatz restaurant – the worst kind, with snooty sommeliers, show-offy menus and rarefied ingredients. Whereas all you need to do is to scale up the ingredients of the dinner you were cooking anyway and lay out another few plates. Stick a candle or twain on the table if you can be bothered, but there is really no need.

1970s and '80s television cook Keith Floyd had the right idea about entertaining: 'There is no mystery. Careful shopping, fresh ingredients and an unhurried approach are nearly all you need. There is one more thing – love. Love for food and love for those you invite to your table.' When preparing for dinner guests, advised Floyd, don't go shopping with a list of ingredients for a specific dish; go shopping with an open mind and be prepared to cook something else entirely if one of your ingredients isn't in season.

Food and seduction have always made cosy bedfellows for chaps. From simmering stews by candlelight to optimistically pre-prepared breakfasts in bed – see Chapter 1 for advice on both optimistic and pessimistic breakfasts – every fellow knows that a lady loves to be cooked for. Regaling a paramour with the delights of one's favourite little bistro is useful at the beginning of a courtship, but serving her a home-cooked venison stew signals a much more desirable form of eligibility.

And what would a chap have to say about etiquette in the contemporary world? Perhaps he would concur with the advice given by Edward Turner in *The Young Man's Companion* (1866): 'Never at any time, whether at a formal or a familiar dinner party, commit the impropriety of talking to a servant: nor even address any remark about one of them to one of the party. Nothing can be more ill-bred. You merely ask for what you want in a grave and civil tone, and wait with patience until your order is obeyed.'

Absolutely not – far better to follow the example of Edward VII, who, while entertaining a well-known guest from India observed that, when consuming asparagus, his guest was hurling the discarded stems over his shoulder on to the floor. Without batting an eyelid, his majesty followed suit, and the rest of the party soon joined in, all throwing their asparagus stems on the floor.

As our dining habits have evolved, so have our notions of etiquette. Today, far more common causes of dinner table discomfort are whether to accept the last sausage on a serving dish or whether to help oneself to a top-up from the wine bottle. In the absence of rules of etiquette, we have made up new ones of our own, just to ensure that meals are

---

Today, far more common causes of dinner table discomfort are whether to accept the last sausage on a serving dish or whether to help oneself to a top-up from the wine bottle.

---

conducted with enough snobbery and awkwardness to make us feel like we're in a restaurant. No need for any of that nonsense, as we will explain in between the recipes in this book.

Cooking for Chaps is not designed for the reader to give posh dinner parties as a novelty. Overall, these are recipes for perfectly practical meals for any time of the day or evening. We will not be instructing you to go and purchase a bottle of very costly extra virgin olive oil and vegetables in baby sizes; you will, however, be given a list of much cheaper stores with which to fill your pantry that will ultimately aid you to create many of our recipes.

Where possible, we have indicated which particular season is the most likely to yield the produce required from the shortest distance from your home. In this way, our recipes will encourage the purchase of local victuals, as well as satisfying the palates of a nation that has become rather difficult to impress. So, rather than trying to foist on you the cuisine of a South Sea Island you have never heard of, we offer you the cuisine of Great Britain that you have never heard of – and we guarantee your taste-buds will be pleasantly surprised.

– Gustav Temple and
Clare Gabbett-Mulhallen, 2014

KITCHEN EQUIPMENT

- Large, sharp, good-quality chopping knife

- Good, chunky, wooden chopping board – not one made of plastic, nylon, glass or anything silly

- Several rolls of baking parchment. Don't bother with greaseproof paper; baking parchment will always serve in its stead.

- Rolling pin (or you can improvise with a straight-sided bottle, such as a Claret wine bottle)

- Long, strong aluminium foil

- Clingfilm

- Kitchen scissors – for cutting up and cutting out

- A round or square cake tin, or you can use a tin with a lid, i.e. a biscuit tin – you can bake and store a cake in this

- Baking dish

- Ovenproof casserole with a lid

- Individual ramekins or other small, ovenproof dishes

- One large heavy-bottomed frying pan

- One small heavy-bottomed frying pan

- Small sauce whisk

- Large balloon whisk

- Magimix food processor, or hand-held stick blender with a chopping gadget

- A couple of large mixing bowls – a clean washing-up bowl will do if that's all you have

- One small, one medium, one large saucepan – with lids

- Large high-sided roasting tin with metal trivet

- A few wooden spoons

- Measuring spoons

TEASPOONS AND TABLESPOONS

Teaspoons and tablespoons, often the only measurements used in old-fashioned recipe books, are nearly always smaller than you think. A proper teaspoon measure is 5ml, which is actually the size of one of those plastic measuring spoons that come with a bottle of cough mixture. So if you are using a normal household teaspoon, have a good look at it compared to the medicine spoon. A proper tablespoon measures 15ml: ensure you don't use a serving spoon by mistake, which is much larger. If you don't have a proper set of measuring spoons, just use 3 teaspoons for 1 tablespoon and you will have the correct amount. And try to develop a cough so that you have to buy some medicine and get the spoon.

ESSENTIALS

STORE CUPBOARD

Plain flour
Self-raising flour
Baking powder
Bicarbonate of soda
Panko breadcrumbs
Porridge oats
Soft brown sugar
Caster sugar
Demerara sugar
Icing sugar
Golden syrup
Treacle
Vanilla extract
Good-quality stock cubes

SPICES

Sea salt flakes – Maldon
Fine sea salt for baking
Black peppercorns for grinding
Ground mace
Ground cinnamon
Saffron
Whole nutmegs

CANS AND PRESERVES

Chestnuts – vacuum-packed or canned
Artichokes – canned or frozen
Truffles in oil
Dried wild mushrooms
Canned oysters
Jars of cockles in brine
Worcestershire sauce
Selection of mustards, including Colman's
    mustard powder
Mushroom ketchup
Cans or jars of anchovies in oil
Anchovy paste
Gentlemen's Relish
Beef consommé

OILS AND VINEGARS

Sunflower oil or groundnut oil
Rapeseed oil
Good-quality cider and red wine vinegar

FROM THE GARDEN

Lovage plant
Small bay tree
Thyme plant

IN THE FRIDGE

Butter – you can use any sort, salted or
    unsalted, as long as it's real butter
Goose fat
Good, fresh, large eggs
Fresh cream – double or whipping
Stilton
Other good-quality hard cheese, such as
    Cheddar
Milk – full fat
Good bacon

IN THE FREEZER

Peas
Broad beans
Spinach – leaf, not chopped

FRESH FRUIT AND VEGETABLES

Lemons
Onions
Shallots
Carrots
Celery
Little Gem lettuce

BREAKFAST DRINKS

BUCK'S FIZZ

Buck's Club was one of the better gentlemen's clubs in London, founded in 1919 by Captain Herbert Buckmaster. Head barman at the club was Mr McGarry, who invented what we know today as Buck's Fizz – essentially one-part champagne to two-parts orange juice – and also added a third, secret, ingredient whose identity only the barmen at Buck's Club know. The drink was created to allow members to drink in the morning without it being too obvious. The fact that Buck's Fizz is served in a champagne glass somewhat undermined this subterfuge.

JEEVES' HANGOVER CURE

'I would have clutched at anything that looked like a lifeline that morning. I swallowed the stuff. For a moment I felt as if somebody had touched off a bomb inside the old bean and was strolling down my throat with a lighted torch, and then everything seemed suddenly to get all right. The sun shone in through the window; birds twittered in the tree-tops; and, generally speaking, hope dawned once more.' Thus did Bertie Wooster recount the magical effects of the hangover cure prepared for him by his newly appointed manservant Jeeves. The recipe is described as one raw egg, Worcestershire sauce and 'red' pepper – presumably cayenne. There is no reason for these ingredients to have any curative effect on a hangover, but the effects are likely to be more palliative, and probably far more effective, if the drink is prepared by a highly intelligent gentleman's gentleman.

CHAPTER I

BREAKFAST

The one meal the British are known for is breakfast. Some visitors from foreign parts may even get the impression that all we ever eat is the morning meal, three times a day, and there is not much to disabuse them of this notion. British cafés regularly trumpet the availability of 15 or 20 breakfast menus, yet upon closer inspection are offering an infinite number of variations on the same thing: eggs and bacon with a few canned vegetables leaking all over the plate. Bertie Wooster would be appalled; if in need of some early morning sustenance, he would simply ask Jeeves to throw a couple of kidneys into the pan.

EGGS CUMBERBATCH

The origins of Eggs Benedict are North American, but that needn't prevent us from enjoying the dish and renaming it after one of Britain's finest thespian exports. Served in a glass tumbler, Eggs Cumberbatch are so much more elegant and intimate – ideal for a Sunday breakfast in bed with one's paramour, or presented to houseguests one would like to impress. Just as good, however, is to use individual ramekins for preparing and serving; either way, the eggs are prevented from splodging all over the place and the strong flavours are not allowed to disperse.

EQUIPMENT

1 x glass tumbler or small
    ramekin per person

♦ INGREDIENTS ♦

Serves 1 – multiply up at will

a little butter, for greasing
45g (approx. 3 tablespoons)
    of either shredded ham
    hock, smoked salmon or
    cubes of smoked haddock,
    and/or some cooked spinach
2 tablespoons single cream
1 very fresh egg
salt and freshly ground black
    pepper
toast, hot rolls or Melba Toast,
    to serve

1. Rub butter around the inside of the glass or ramekin.

2. Put the ham, salmon or haddock and/or spinach in the bottom of the glass. Grind over a little pepper and then pour on 1 tablespoon of the cream.

3. Crack in an egg, drizzle with the other tablespoon of cream and sprinkle generously with salt and black pepper.

4. Transfer the glass to a saucepan. Add hot water to come halfway up the sides of the glass, bring to a gentle simmer, and put on the lid, leaving a little gap for steam to escape or water will condense into the glass. Allow to cook for 10–12 minutes until the white is cooked but the yolk still soft.

5. Lift out the glass, dry the sides and place on a napkin on a plate for serving.

6. Serve with toast, hot rolls or Melba toast (see page 24).

DEVILLED KIDNEYS

❝ "To Carbury Manor!" said he, as he ate some devilled kidneys which the cook had been specially ordered to get for his breakfast.' Thus spake Anthony Trollope in *The Way We Live Now*, published in 1875. Sadly, the way we live now is to eschew the hardy innards such as liver and kidneys in favour of stuff found nearer the surface of the animal. All manner of foods were devilled in the nineteenth century, from sausages to mushrooms to mackerel (see page 136), perhaps to smother any lurking traces of bacteria, but also, during winter, to fire up the senses before a morning spent striding across the sward in one's greatcoat.

EQUIPMENT

4 x skewers (optional), soaked in water if using wooden ones. You could also use rosemary twigs stripped of leaves.

◆ INGREDIENTS ◆

Serves 4

8 lambs' kidneys
2 tablespoons mustard powder
2 tablespoons Worcestershire sauce
sea salt and freshly ground black pepper
hot buttered toast and freshly chopped flat-leaf parsley (optional), to serve

① Using a sharp knife, halve the kidneys lengthways on a chopping board, and remove and discard the cores.

② To make the devilling sauce: mix together the mustard powder and Worcestershire sauce in a medium bowl. Put the kidneys in the bowl and turn over until coated in the sauce – this can be done up to 24 hours ahead. Season with a good pinch of sea salt and plenty of freshly ground black pepper.

③ Preheat grill to hot.

④ Thread 4 kidney halves onto each skewer (if using). Arrange on grill pan and grill on each side for 3–4 minutes.

⑤ Serve with hot buttered toast and sprinkled with freshly chopped flat-leaf parsley, if using.

LAYING THE BREAKFAST TRAY

First of all, ensure it's your best tray: wooden and with sides of a decent height. Lay it with, ideally, a linen napkin (never a 'serviette'), silver cutlery (mismatched is fine), and a sprig of something from the garden in a very small, unpretentious vase, with the breakfast itself served on perhaps the single example you have of your finest crockery – no matter if you don't have the set any longer because your guest will only see the one plate. If you haven't got a linen napkin, use a good tea-towel (not one with the recipe for a Cornish pasty on it) but do iron it first.

THE COLONEL'S KEDGEREE

Spicy or Fruity

The original version of kedgeree was discovered by English travellers in India and Persia in about 1680. *Kitchri*, as it was named, was a rice dish served as an accompaniment to fish; it actually contained no fish. The first we hear of fish being added to the rice dish is in Eliza Acton's *Modern Cookery for Private Families* (1845), but we turned to Colonel Kenney-Herbert for the recipe, because he wrote a book entitled *Fifty Breakfasts*, so he must have known what he was talking about. As the Colonel says, you can have both your fish and rice ready prepared; kedgeree is a great dish for using up leftovers. Or at least you may have boiled the rice and cooked the fish while making lunch or dinner the day before.

◆ INGREDIENTS ◆

Serves 4

For the spicy version
450g fish (fresh or salted –
    we like smoked haddock)
3 eggs
75g butter
1 shallot, finely chopped
175g cooked Basmati rice
pinch of turmeric
small bunch of soft herbs –
    flat-leaf parsley, chervil
    (slightly aniseedy), dill,
    chives (slightly oniony) or
    lovage, chopped or snipped
    with scissors (optional)
1 lemon or orange, cut into
    segments, to serve

For the fruity version
As above, plus:
1 large apple, peeled and grated
2 tablespoons sultanas
pinch of cinnamon

Kedgeree: Spiced version

1. If the fish is not cooked, place in a baking dish (no need to cover or wrap in foil) and bake at 180°C/gas mark 4 for 15 minutes. Let it cool, peel away any skin and break into large chunks. Remove bones.

2. To hard-boil the eggs: put them into a small pan and cover with cold water. Bring to the boil and cook for 6 minutes. Plunge into cold water and run the cold tap on them constantly until they are cool. Peel and chop roughly or quarter.

3. Melt the butter in a frying pan over a low heat, add the shallot and fry gently until softened. Keeping the heat fairly low, add the cooked rice, fish and turmeric. Go easy on the turmeric – you don't want your kedgeree looking radioactive. Stir carefully (avoid breaking up the fish too much) to combine and heat through. Season to taste. Add the chopped boiled eggs and turn into a very hot dish for serving.

4. Straying slightly from the Colonel's recipe, you can add some fresh chopped soft herbs to the dish. Serve it with chunks of lemon or orange for your guests to add themselves.

Kedgeree: Fruited version

1. Either add the apple and sultanas to the mixture above, or use them in place of the shallot. Fry the fruit gently in the melted butter as you would the shallot and continue as above, adding a pinch of turmeric and a pinch of cinnamon. The flavours are further heightened if you use chopped lovage, which adds a slight curry/savoury flavour, and serve with orange segments for squeezing over the finished dish.

Olde English
MARMALADE
◼ IN A JIFFY ◼

No need to wash out old jam jars and make fiddly frilly covers. For the vessel, just use anything clean you would eat off – a jam jar if you like, but any little pot or dish will do. Those little glass whatsits that people bung nightlights in also work a treat, and can also be used to serve the marmalade on the breakfast-in-bed tray.

◆ INGREDIENTS ◆

1 orange – not Seville
160g (approx.) sugar –
   granulated or caster is fine

① Wash the orange. Using a vegetable peeler, peel away all the zest (the coloured part of the skin), trying not to take too much pith – a little is good for flavour.

② Using a jolly sharp knife, cut the pieces of zest into very small slices – matchstick thin. Put into a bowl.

③ Now peel off and discard the pith from the orange either using your fingers or, if you've got a tricky blighter, a sharp knife.

④ Chop the orange up, removing the pips as you go. It's much easier to slice it into rings first, pile them up and then hack through it with a large chopping knife. Try to catch all the juice. Add the lot to the bowl with the zest.

⑤ Weigh the mixture and make a note of the weight. Weigh out an equal weight of sugar. Add the sugar to the mixture along with 3 tablespoons water. Transfer to a saucepan set over a low heat and stir gently until the sugar dissolves. Once dissolved, increase the heat and boil for approx. 10 minutes. Stir regularly to avoid burning. The marmalade is ready when it is thick enough for a spoon to clear a path when it is scraped along the bottom of the pan.

⑥ Pour the marmalade into your chosen receptacle. Keep in the fridge and eat within 2 weeks.

PORRIDGE
THREE VERSIONS

As sure as eggs is eggs, there will be days, particularly horrid winter days, when you feel like something longer lasting in your belly than a hen's egg or twain. But before you start reaching for the Ready Brek, or even the milk, which will almost certainly burn if you make porridge with it, hold fire! All you really need to make porridge is water, porridge oats and a little time. We've given you three options here, of varying speeds – but the overnight version is truly worth it, when you see your guests cooing over the breakfast table. If you really want to impress them, serve the porridge in the proper Scottish way, with a glass of cold milk next to the bowl of hot porridge. You spoon out a bit of thick porridge, then dip the spoon into the cold milk and deliver to the mouth.

♦ INGREDIENTS ♦

Serves 2

1 cup porridge oats
3 cups water
salt, sugar, syrup, treacle or
    cream, to serve

Quick method
Combine the oats and 3 cups of water in a bowl and stir. Zap in microwave for 2 minutes, stir, and zap for another 2 minutes, then let stand for 2 minutes.

Slower method
Put the oats and 3 cups water in a small saucepan and stir well while cooking over a very low heat (unsoaked porridge has a tendency to stick). This will take 15–20 minutes – the slower, the better.

Overnight method
Stir together the oats and 3 cups water in a small saucepan. Allow them to soak overnight. Next morning, put the pan over a low heat on the hob and allow to cook gently for 30 minutes or so, stirring occasionally. You can add extra water as you go along. Before serving, let the porridge stand off the heat with the lid on – it stops the porridge sticking.

Serve with salt, sugar, syrup, etc. as you wish. Some also like a little cream drizzled over the top.

Remember to fill the empty pan with cold water to make it easier to wash up.

The Cranachan Awakes

Cranachan is an ancient recipe from the wilds of the Scottish Highlands. Traditionally all the ingredients were brought separately to the table and assembled by each guest in a tall glass, according to taste. This is an unfussy recipe so measurements needn't be exact. You could soak half the oats overnight in whisky and provide both alcoholic and non-alcoholic versions. Guests will be further impressed if you break into a spirited rendition of 'The Bonnie Hoose o'Airlie' while serving. *Note: if any actual Scots are present, it is probably wise to omit this detail.*

◆ INGREDIENTS ◆

Serves 1; multiply at will

1 ½ tablespoons porridge oats
   or rolled oats
150ml yogurt or yogurt
   with a bit of cream added
1 tablespoon honey (runny not
   set, but use the good stuff
   – it tastes better)
1 tablespoon whisky (optional)
small handful raspberries
   – blackberries are good too

① Toast the oats in a dry frying pan or saucepan over a medium heat. Keep stirring all the while; it only takes a couple of minutes. Toasted oats have more flavour and a crunchier texture. You can keep them in a jar or freezer bag in the fridge.

② In the morning, add the ingredients in layers in a tall glass. Otherwise, place them all in dishes on the table and allow your guests to assemble their own.

BREAKFAST ETIQUETTE

While there is no specific dress code for breakfast (you would normally expect everyone to be dressed for whatever activity in which they are partaking after breakfast, be it hunting, shooting, fishing or going for a walk), there are certain rules regarding nightwear. Male house guests descending to breakfast in their pyjamas may do so only if covered by a silk dressing gown. This should have been packed in their overnight bag and is not provided by the host. They should also be wearing velvet slippers – bare feet are not acceptable; flip-flops definitely not.

Ladies may not take breakfast in their nightgowns, even if covered by a dressing gown. This may seem a trifle imbalanced, but gentlemen's nightwear is much less revealing than ladies', and it wouldn't be fair on the staff, nor indeed the other male guests, to have too much female flesh on display behind the kippers. Pipes may be smoked after breakfast but only with the full permission of the host/ess. The better country houses will have a special room for this.

BREAKFAST IN BED

The Paramour Version

We have provided two versions of this laconic meal, the first aimed at lovers lingering in the boudoir on a Sunday morning. A chap will not wish to busy himself too long in the kitchen, allowing his lady-love to make one of two fatal decisions: one, to arise and get dressed; or two, even worse, to root around in the bedside table and discover a sheaf of poems dedicated to various other ladies' ankles. Some of the preparation may be done the evening before, but if that evening was spent persuading said female to come back to one's domicile, even then a chap should not be detained in the kitchen for longer than 15 minutes.

◆ INGREDIENTS ◆

Serves 2

For the lemon butter
100g unsalted butter at room temperature
zest of ¼ lemon and 1 teaspoon juice
pinch of salt and white pepper

200g smoked salmon slices
1 lemon, quartered and any obvious pips removed
4 slices bread
freshly ground black or white pepper
1 bottle Champagne, chilled, to serve

① To make the lemon butter: put the soft butter into a small mixing bowl and beat it with a wooden spoon or whisk to get it really soft. Add the lemon zest and juice, a pinch of salt and white pepper and combine. Put on clingfilm or baking parchment and roll up to form a log. Chill the log for about 15 minutes to firm up.

② Run a fork down the sides of the log to make a nice filigree pattern if you wish. Cut the log into coins approx. 1cm thick. If you like a personal design, stamp your signet ring into the butter. Keep the butter cool but do not return it to the fridge.

③ Now lay the smoked salmon on a plate, adding lemon quarters, and sprinkle over a grind of black or white pepper. Prepare the tray: glass of Champagne, flower, knife, napkin, plate with smoked salmon, small butter dish with a few coins of lemon butter.

④ Preheat the grill to medium or the oven to 190°C/ gas mark 5. Make Melba Toast by toasting the bread under the grill or in a toaster until lightly golden, then cut off the crusts. Slide the bread knife horizontally into the centre of each slice. Cut straight through, to give 2 very thin slices, then cut each one in half diagonally. Place the slices, untoasted sides uppermost, under the preheated grill or oven for a few moments.

⑤ Put the Melba toast into a toast rack, place on the tray and saunter into the boudoir, ready to lap up the lavish praise.

BREAKFAST IN BED

The House Guest Version

This fortifying dish would also work perfectly well in the previous scenario, but may be more suited to feeding a house guest, or even provided as a gentle palliative to a relative a tad under the weather. The egg-boiling process requires precision timing, and is not something you want to take your chances with while a pulchritudinous lady awaits you in your four-poster. The Twiglet toast, as invented by Clare's childhood friend Sophie Embleton, provides a fiery and fortifying companion to the boiled eggs, and will revive not only a maiden aunt suffering from lumbago, but also the victim of even the most ferocious hangover. Some magical alchemical process takes place when you heat Bovril past a certain point; luckily, foreigners have never discovered this, which is why Bovril has never appeared on the shelves of any country other than Britain.

♦ I N G R E D I E N T S ♦

Serves 2

2 eggs

For the Twiglet toast
4 slices bread
50g butter
Bovril, to taste

(1) Get the breakfast tray ready and warm the plates by keeping them in very hot water for a few minutes.

(2) To boil eggs perfectly, ideally start with the eggs at room temperature. For soft-boiled, put the eggs into a saucepan and cover with cold water. Bring to the boil and then turn down to simmer for precisely 3 minutes 50 seconds. Drain and keep warm in eggcups with hats.

(3) Meanwhile, to make the Twiglet toast, preheat the grill. Toast the bread lightly on both sides, then butter it well and evenly and spread with a generous layer of Bovril. Return the slices to the grill and allow the Bovril to bubble and blister under the heat, being careful not to burn the crusts.

(4) To serve, cut the Twiglet toast into soldiers and arrange on the (thoroughly dried) plates with the eggcups.

ELEVENSES

The modern age, in its ceaseless quest to make worker hamsters of us all, has gradually eroded the elevenses meal from our lives, in the mistaken belief that it may slow down productivity, especially in offices. Balderdash, we say. A man or woman fortified with a glass of Bullshot or Newmarket Cobbler (see recipes below) and a plate of Cinnamon Toast or Boiled Fruit Cake (see pages 68 and 69), is ready to tackle any task, even if that task, in the case of full-time chaps, happens to involve dawdling away at practically nothing until lunchtime.

Elevenses should be taken at table (not at one's desk) just like any other meal. Think of it as a meal rather than a snack (the alcohol content will help that). If for some peculiar reason your employer condemns the consumption of alcohol in the morning, then simply take a warming cup of Bovril instead. Of course other things happen at this hour, for example weddings and funerals. The two drinks we describe below are both wonderfully fortifying and restoring. Good for the nerves, and jolly nice to offer to wobbly aunts and nervous grooms en route to ominous events – your own or someone else's.

BULLSHOT:

Bullshot can be made with Fino sherry or vodka, the latter providing more of a tang, while sherry injects a little more tone. Don't get too bogged down by which is superior – the best ingredient is the one you happen to have to hand. If you use sherry, ensure that it is as dry a version as you can get. Please note, Dear Reader, that those labouring under the misconception that Bullshot is two words are, in fact, referring to artifical insemination.

Makes 4 teacups-full

Open a tin of good beef consommé and heat gently in a saucepan (or in the microwave). When hot, remove from heat and add Fino sherry or vodka to taste. Our preferred ratio is 4 parts consommé to 1 part sherry. Serve in china teacups.

NEWMARKET COBBLER:

This liquid reviver of tired souls has come to us via that wonderful country woman Sylvia Stratton, who would drink this after a day's hunting. If ever you find yourself utterly exhausted after a morning's exertions, mix yourself one of these and it will work the same magic as if you had just risen from a blissful, restoring slumber.

Simply mix equal parts gin and sherry (the sweet sort is just the stuff for this) and sip, allowing the warming nuttiness to flow through you like liquid gold.

— CHAPTER 2 —

¡LUNCH!

For many, especially the gainfully employed, lunch can often consist of a sandwich, served in a triangular cardboard carton, hastily gobbled down at an office desk or standing in the rain outside one's workplace, close enough to be hauled back inside if necessary. For chaps, typically 'between jobs', lunch is a meal that allows them to celebrate their idleness. Lunch should be long – at least an hour and a half – and enjoyed seated, accompanied by several bottles of wine or ale, depending on the dish. Neither is there any shame in lunching alone; our recipes work just as easily for one as for twenty guests. Just don't try making a Harry Palmer Omelette outside your office in the rain.

KING OF FISHCAKES

Let's face it, fishcakes do not benefit from the most salubrious image, often perched atop a newspaper cone of chips and boasting minimal fish content. Ours contain plenty of fresh fish (no potato or crumb), and samphire, a classic English vegetable that grows on rocky crags by the sea, earning itself a mention in *King Lear*: 'Half-way down/Hangs one that gathers samphire; dreadful trade!'. You can quote this when serving our fishcakes, or use peas instead of samphire and keep Shakespeare out of the equation. But do include the lemon-saffron clotted cream sauce. If you like the idea of using seaweed but cannot find any samphire, you can use dulse instead, which you can often find dried, or some Japanese nori, which you can buy in dried sheets in the 'World Foods' aisle of the supermarket.

EQUIPMENT

Food-processor (optional)

♦ INGREDIENTS ♦

Serves 4

For the fishcakes
800g any fish, i.e. cod/salmon or a mixture e.g. fish pie mix. If you are a big smoked salmon fan you can substitute 50g smoked salmon
1 egg white
2 tablespoons clotted cream
2 whole spring onions, finely chopped, green parts included
¼ teaspoon mace
90g samphire or 45g frozen peas
butter (if frying)
lots of salt and freshly ground black pepper

For the sauce
5 strands (small pinch) saffron
227g (small pot) clotted cream (minus the 2 tablespoons used above)
zest and juice of ½ lemon

① If baking the fishcakes, preheat oven to 200°C/gas mark 6.

② Put the fish in the food-processor with the egg white, cream, spring onions, mace and salt and pepper. Pulse chop until finely chopped and coming together. If using samphire, add a third (saving the remainder for garnish) and pulse until a little chopped but still visible. If using peas, add them still frozen and stir in until evenly distributed. Tip contents into a large bowl. (If lacking in the gadget department, chop the fish finely with a knife and bind with the other ingredients by stirring thoroughly in a large bowl.)

③ Using an ice-cream scoop or wet hands, scoop a small amount and shape into an even-sized ball – billiard-ball size – then squash slightly with the palm of your hand to make a nice fishcake shape. Repeat with the rest of the mixture – it should make 8. If frying, melt a little butter in a pan and fry fishcakes gently on either side for approx. 4 minutes per side. If baking, arrange on a baking tray or roasting tin and bake for 12–15 minutes – no need to turn them.

④ To cook the remaining samphire, fry gently in butter for a few minutes, alongside the fishcakes if you like.

⑤ To make the sauce: put a couple of strands of saffron into a mug and pour on 2 teaspoons boiling water. Stir to release colour and flavour. Put the clotted cream into a bowl, pour on the saffron mixture plus lemon zest and juice and a pinch of salt. Stir well. You can make this up to 2 days before and leave covered in the fridge, as the flavours will infuse. Serve 2 fishcakes per person and serve with the sauce and samphire (if using).

MEAT STEW TWO WAYS
The pink and the brown version

There are two fundamental methods of cooking a stew – one by browning the meat first, and one by not doing so. The other factor is whether or not to add flour to thicken your stew. Some prefer not to, which creates a liquid rather like a stock. Others add flour and end up with a thicker sauce, more like a gravy. Choose your stew depending on the time of year and how much time you have. In a dash? Then go pink. All the time in the world? Go brown, old chap. The first of these is the quicker version: meat goes in uncooked. We have provided quantities for 4 people – if you are dining solo (and why not?), you can freeze the remainder or it will keep happily in the fridge for up to three days.

◆ INGREDIENTS ◆

Serves 4

450g whole piece top rump, braising steak, skirt steak beef or braising cuts of lamb, cut into approx. 3cm pieces
2 onions or shallots, cut into eighths
2 large carrots, peeled and cut into chunks
2 small turnips, peeled and cut into chunks
2 large potatoes, peeled and cut into chunks
3 tablespoons pearl barley (optional) – add an extra 50ml liquid if using
2 bay leaves
2 juniper berries
1 teaspoon whole black peppercorns
dash of Worcestershire sauce (optional)
small squeeze of anchovy paste (optional)
350ml wine, ale or Guinness
salt and freshly ground black pepper

THE PINK VERSION

EQUIPMENT

➤ 1.5 litre casserole dish or ovenproof saucepan or large Pyrex bowl with foil as a lid; you can balance a baking tray on top for extra coverage

① Sprinkle the meat all over with a little salt and pepper. Put the meat and all the other ingredients into the casserole dish/pan/bowl. Add cold water just to cover. Put on the lid and chuck in the oven at either 140°C/gas mark 2 for 6 hours or 180°C/gas mark 4 for 2 hours. If you only have a hob – cook on the slowest setting for 4 hours with the lid on, but do check and add extra water if the level drops dramatically.

② Check for seasoning and adjust before serving.

THE BROWN VERSION

Ingredients as opposite, except:
3 tablespoons goose fat
450g braising steak, cut into
    approx. 3cm pieces
100g plain flour, seasoned -
    you won't need it all

E Q U I P M E N T

Heavy-bottomed large oven-proof casserole or saucepan

(1) Preheat oven to 180°C/gas mark 4 (or you can cook on the hob).

(2) Put your stew pan over the heat with 2 tablespoons of the goose fat and get it really hot.

(3) Dip each piece of steak into the flour and shake off the excess. Brown a few pieces at a time in the hot fat, turning them over – you are just colouring them a lovely brown, not cooking the meat through.

(4) Melt the remainder of the fat in the pan over a medium heat, add the vegetables, pearl barley (if using), browned meat, herbs, spices, seasoning and Worcestershire sauce or anchovy paste (if using). Stir well to mix the flavours for a couple of minutes. Pour in whichever liquid you are using plus enough water to cover. Put on the lid and cook in the oven for 2 hours or simmer very gently on the hob for 2 hours.

(5) Remember to check the seasoning before serving.

If there are leftovers, you could transfer them to a smaller dish, cover with mashed potato or root vegetables and bake in the oven for about 20 minutes to make a lovely new dish.

DOUGH-EYED
CHICKEN STEW

One day, you may find yourself holed up in a rented farmhouse in Cornwall during the hols with a gang of cronies, among them a charming young thing called Daisy whom you'd like to impress. It's your turn to cook lunch, everybody wants something nice and fortifying with a bit of a zing to keep out the cold – and Daisy happens to be a big fan of chicken. Only snag is, it's midday, you've only just arisen and everyone expects a decent lunch in the next half an hour. Time to bring out the big guns and tackle our 'fake' chicken stew with crusty, mustardy dumplings, which actually only takes about 20 minutes to cook.

♦ INGREDIENTS ♦

Serves 4

1 stock cube, either chicken or
    vegetable, or use 600ml real stock
a good slosh of white wine –
    about 50ml
2 teaspoons fresh or dried tarragon,
    chervil or parsley (or a mixture of
    all three)
1 bay leaf
1 teaspoon mushroom ketchup
½ teaspoon anchovy paste
3 large carrots, chopped or sliced
    approx. 1cm thick
1 leek, white part only, finely sliced
3 skinless chicken breasts or 8
    thighs, cut into 2cm chunks
1 mug frozen peas/broad beans
    (optional)
1 Little Gem lettuce, sliced
    horizontally or equivalent quantity
    of watercress, roughly chopped
salt and freshly ground black pepper

For the dumplings
100g self-raising flour
50g suet
2 tablespoons grainy mustard

EQUIPMENT

Food processor (optional)

① Using water from the hot tap to hurry things along, put 600ml water in a large saucepan over a high heat. Chuck in the stock cube, wine, some black pepper (no need for salt if you're using a stock cube), herbs, bay leaf, mushroom ketchup and anchovy paste. Give it a good stir, and taste to ensure it has a balanced flavour. Toss in the carrots and leek as you chop them. Keep the heat at a good simmer.

② To make the dumplings: put the flour, suet and mustard into a mixing bowl or food-processor. Season with salt and pepper, stir around to incorporate, add 75ml water and mix quickly to make a very soft sticky dough. Wet your hands (stops the mixture sticking to you) and, taking small pieces – about golf-ball size – form little balls and set aside.

③ Toss the chicken into the saucepan, and add the peas/ broad beans (if using) and lettuce/watercress, give it a stir. Finally, add the dumplings. Put a lid on it and leave to bubble for 10 minutes.

④ The dumplings will be lovely and fluffy. Taste the liquid for seasoning before serving with crusty bread.

HORSERADISH
TOAD IN THE HOLE

While the origins of Toad in the Hole, like Pan Haggerty, are shrouded in mystery, with theories varying from the dish's similarity to a toad peeping out of the mud (really?) to it being a corruption of 'Turd in the Hole' (charming!), there is no doubt that everyone likes a nice sausage surrounded by Yorkshire pudding, smothered with lashings of onion gravy. Traditionally, Toad in the Hole was made from chunks of leftover meat rather than sausages, which creates a delicious seepage of flavour into the batter. Either way, your guests are in for a heart-warming trip down the cobbled streets of yesteryear. Serve wearing a flat cap.

EQUIPMENT

Roasting tin, or anything metal; it conducts the heat better and faster
Blender/food-processor (optional)

♦ INGREDIENTS ♦

Serves 4

12 very good sausages
225g self-raising flour
3 eggs
2 tablespoons horseradish – pure horseradish, not mixed with cream
approx. 500ml milk (use full fat)
1 tablespoon goose fat or beef dripping – at a push, use vegetable oil
salt and white pepper

(1) Preheat oven to 180°C/gas mark 4.

(2) Roast the sausages in the metal tin – you don't need extra fat as they make their own and, above all, don't prick them – until nicely browned; approx. 25 minutes. Take out of the oven and turn up the heat to 220°C/gas mark 7.

(3) Meanwhile, make the batter: combine the flour, eggs, and horseradish in a bowl. Season, add milk and whisk until smooth. Or, put all the ingredients in a blender and whizz until smooth. The result should be a creamy, pouring consistency like double cream. Add more milk if necessary.

(4) Add the goose fat or dripping to the roasting tin, along with the sausages, and return to the oven for a couple of minutes to get really hot.

(5) Wearing oven gloves and working quickly, pull the oven rack/roasting tin out halfway and pour in the batter mixture. Give it a good shake to distribute the batter and get it under the sausages. Shove it back into the oven, shut the door and bake for 15–20 minutes, until the batter has puffed up and is risen and golden.

(6) Serve immediately at the table, wearing a flat cap if not among Northern folk, accompanied with vegetables (see Chapter 6), mashed potato and more horseradish.

JAMES BOND
CHEESE SOUFFLÉ

James Bond dined exceptionally well at Auric Goldfinger's place. Each re-reading of that book seems to reveal more and more items being delivered to the captured secret agent's table. Perhaps he thought it would be a last supper, or perhaps Fleming was just showing off what a gourmet he was. Bond orders a cheese soufflé as a savoury for dessert, but you can just as easily serve this as a light lunch dish. This soufflé is made instantly easier for you by baking it in a soup plate and not a ramekin – so you don't have to worry about it rising or sinking. The secret is to use room temperature eggs and a hot oven and baking tray to give an immediate fiery whoosh to your soufflé.

EQUIPMENT

1 ovenproof soup plate

◆ INGREDIENTS ◆

Serves 1

20g butter
20g plain flour
75ml full-fat milk
50g cheese or mixture of
    cheeses (use strongly
    flavoured varieties such
    as mature Cheddar), grated –
    reserve half to sprinkle over
    the top
a grating of nutmeg
1 teaspoon thyme leaves
2 eggs at room temperature,
    separated
½ lemon
salt and freshly ground black
    pepper

TIP: Do not whisk your egg whites too stiff. You will make it impossible to fold them into the cheese mixture. They should be thick and creamy but not dry. Always add a drop or two of something acidic to help strengthen the whites – a squeeze of lemon usually does the trick.

① Preheat oven to 200°C/gas mark 6 and place a baking tray on the middle shelf.

② Put the butter, flour and milk into a saucepan over a medium heat. Cook until boiling, stirring constantly with a whisk to prevent lumps. Simmer for a couple of minutes until thick and glossy. Stir in half the cheese, the nutmeg and thyme and season. Pour the mixture into a large mixing bowl. You can complete this stage up to a day ahead if you like. If you are keeping the mixture, prevent a skin forming by pouring a little melted butter over the surface and pressing a damp sheet of baking parchment, scrunched and unfurled, onto the surface.

③ Room temperature whites whisk up much better so try to remember to get the eggs out of the fridge a couple of hours before you need them. You are aiming to get both mixtures to the same consistency, which makes them much easier to fold together easily.

④ Wipe around the inside of a medium bowl with the lemon half. The lemon juice will help the whites to beat up well. Put in the egg whites and pinch of salt. Start beating on a slow setting to break up the whites, increase speed and whisk until peaks form and you can hold the bowl upside down without the eggs falling out. Don't overwhisk.

⑤ Using the same beaters, add the yolks to the cheese mixture and whisk together, and beat in a tablespoon of the egg whites to loosen the mixture.

⑥ Using a large metal spoon, fold the egg whites into the mixture, a third at time. Gently tip the mixture into the soup plate without knocking the air out, sprinkle with the rest of the cheese and bake for 12–15 minutes. Serve immediately.

SQUIRE'S BAKED ONIONS

There is something quintessentially British about an onion. Reassuringly simple, yet bursting with flavour and complexity, they were the staple, along with bread and cheese, of the British ploughman from the twelfth century, usually carried in the pocket of whatever rustic coat was fashionable at the time. The classic onion as we know it today, as opposed to the shallot, the spring onion or the tree onion, is actually known as the Spanish Onion. Baked, it is a simple country dish all of its own, or can make an eye-catching vegetable portion when served with a heavy meat dish. Don't put them in the pocket of your jacket, though.

EQUIPMENT

Heavy, lidded casserole dish

◆ INGREDIENTS ◆

Serves 2–4, depending on greed

4 large onions
50g butter
1 tin beef consommé
1 small glass port (approx.
    150ml, or more if you are
    fond of it)
sprig of rosemary, plus more
    to garnish
salt and freshly ground black
    pepper

For cheesy breadcrumbs
60g fresh breadcrumbs
100g any hard cheese, grated
good scraping of nutmeg
50g butter, melted

(1) If you intend to bake the onions, preheat oven to 180°C/ gas mark 4.

(2) Leaving the root and skin on the onions, cut off the top of each one and quarter.

(3) Arrange the onions, cut end uppermost, to fit snugly in a heavy casserole dish, supporting one another. Top each onion with a knob of butter, and sprinkle with salt and pepper. Pour around the consommé, fill the tin with water and add that, too. Next pour around the port and add rosemary. Put on the lid and bake for 1 hour or simmer on the hob for 1 hour.

(4) Meanwhile, make the cheesy crumbs. Combine the breadcrumbs, cheese, nutmeg and melted butter in a bowl. Season with salt and pepper.

(5) After approx. 40 minutes, lift the casserole lid and tip the breadcrumb mixture over the onions. Bake, uncovered, for 20 minutes until the crumbs are golden brown. Alternatively, grill for approx. 10 minutes until golden.

(6) Serve the onions – one or two per person – garnished with rosemary, spooning the liquor. Eat with crusty bread.

PAN HAGGERTY

Pan Haggerty is one of those dishes that ought to have some amazing story associated with it, for example, soldiers being nursed back to health on the battlefield during the Crimean War with a dish comprised of what was in their knapsacks (or something). Sorry to disappoint, but all we know about Pan Haggerty is that its origins are from Northumberland and it's bloody delicious. The one sure thing about Pan Haggerty is that you should serve it in the dish in which it was cooked, as you should with anything that originated in the homesteads of simple, rustic folk.

EQUIPMENT

Box grater or food-processor

♦ INGREDIENTS ♦

Serves 2 hungry people

100g butter
3 slices bacon (any sort), cut into lardons
2 large potatoes, peeled and very thinly sliced on a box grater or using a food-processor
2 large onions, thinly sliced in rings
300ml hot chicken stock or wine – any sort you have handy
100g cheese, grated – Red Leicester is jolly good in Pan Haggerty, but any hard cheese will do the job

① Melt the butter in a medium frying pan over a low heat. Add the bacon and fry until crisp. Take the bacon out of the pan and set aside.

② Make a layer of potatoes in the pan, overlapping them slightly. Top with a layer of onions and sprinkle over half the bacon. Repeat with the remaining potatoes, onions and bacon.

③ Pour over the hot stock or wine and allow to bubble away, uncovered, on a medium–low heat for around 35–40 minutes, until soft when stabbed with a sharp knife. The liquid will boil away and the bottom layer will be a little crisp, but don't let it burn.

④ Preheat grill. Sprinkle the cheese over the top of the dish and place under the grill to brown (protect handle as necessary). Very good eaten with something green and crunchy on the side.

HARRY PALMER OMELETTE

There is a wonderful scene in *The Ipcress File*, in which, to show what a gourmet his character Harry Palmer is, Michael Caine declares to his co-star: 'I am going to cook you the best meal you have ever tasted in your life.' We then see him busying himself in the kitchen, breaking two eggs with one hand to show off. During filming, Caine found it impossible to perform this trick, so the hands we see on screen are in fact those of Len Deighton, author of the book of *The Ipcress File* and such a keen cook himself that he penned his own cookbook, *Len Deighton's Action Cook Book*. In our recipe, we have been faithful to Harry Palmer, but, if you prefer, a James Bond version would feature truffles.

◆ INGREDIENTS ◆

Serves 2 – multiply at will

For the filling:
40g butter
½ onion, fairly finely chopped
½ green pepper, deseeded and
chopped lengthwise
150g good quality ham, the
boiled sort, chopped into
1cm squares

For the omelette:
4 large eggs, lightly whisked
60g butter
salt and freshly ground black
pepper

Other good omelette fillings
Devilled kidneys (see page 16)
A few cooked asparagus spears
Cheese – any sort
Smoked haddock with chives
and a few croûtons stuffed
down a slit in the centre
Cockles
Brown shrimp
Smoked oysters
Chopped soft herbs
Stilton and slices of ripe pear

---

① Put a couple of plates in a low oven to warm up. We don't see what Harry does with his omelette in the film, but it is likely to be the following:

② Melt half the butter in a frying pan and cook the onion and green pepper until softened. Take your time over this, as the flavour will be mellower and more delicious. Take them out of the pan. Wipe the pan with kitchen paper.

③ Break the eggs into a bowl, season with salt and pepper and whisk to break up the eggs and get some air bubbles into the mixture – but don't overwhisk.

④ Make one omelette at a time. Put half the butter in the pan, turn up the heat and warm the butter until it is foaming and has a nutty aroma.

⑤ Tip in half the egg mixture – it will start to set on the base immediately. Using your fork, swirl the cooked egg from the bottom of the pan, allowing the uncooked egg to seep though and cook. This is how to make your omelette fluffy.

⑥ Cook the omelette for a maximum of 2 minutes. The surface will be very soft and undercooked – it continues to cook out of the pan. Quickly scatter half the ham pieces evenly over the top and roll up the omelette and tip onto a plate. Make a slit in the top of the rolled omelette and stuff with half the onion and pepper mixture. Transfer to one of the plates in the oven to keep warm, wipe out the pan and repeat the process for the second omelette. Serve immediately.

SALT O' THE EARTH
SHEPHERD'S PIE

The cottage pie/shepherd's pie debate is easily settled by the fact that shepherds tend sheep, so theirs is the one with lamb in it. Cottage pie is the same dish, though predating shepherd's pie by a hundred years, and made with beef instead of lamb. Traditionally made from leftovers from a roast, you can do this if you have half a kilo of beef or lamb left over (unlikely if you had guests). This is why you'll need to bump it up with some fresh mince. We've added lots of classic English root vegetables because they give an earthy flavour to this, the ultimate of English country dishes.

EQUIPMENT

Electric whisk

◆ INGREDIENTS ◆

Serves 2

50g butter, plus extra for the
    topping
1 onion, fairly finely chopped
3 carrots, chopped into chunks
    approx. 3cm
2 sticks celery, finely chopped,
    or ¼ celeriac, peeled and
    chopped into 3cm chunks
450g really good lean minced
    lamb (5 per cent fat); get your
    butcher to mince it from a piece
    of meat you choose
2 glasses red wine (approx. 350ml,
    but slosh in as much as you like)
2 bay leaves
500ml chicken, vegetable or veal
    stock – or stock cube and water
150g frozen petits pois (optional)
500g serving Chap's Mashed
    Potatoes (see page 114)
salt and freshly ground black
    pepper

*Fun things to add for extra flavour if
    you have them: a dash of anchovy
    paste, sherry, mushroom ketchup,
    Worcestershire sauce*

① Melt the butter in a large saucepan or ovenproof casserole. Add the onion, carrots, celery/celeriac and give it all a good stir. Let it sweat away over a low heat while you deal with the meat.

② Get a frying pan hot – don't bother putting in any fat. Put in the lamb and fry it really hard to brown off the meat. Get it as brown and crispy as you can – this creates great flavour and will reward you in spades.

③ Next, add the wine and let it bubble while you scrape up all the lovely bits stuck to the bottom of the pan. Tip the whole caboodle into the pot of veg. Add the bay leaves, stock and any fun flavourings you wish to add, then season.

④ Check the meat mixture for seasoning and adjust accordingly. If you are using peas, now is the time to add them. Just dump them in frozen; they will defrost in a minute. This way they stay nice and bright green.

⑤ If you are not using a fancy oven-to-table dish, pile the lot into a pretty baking dish that will look good on the table for your guests, put the hot mash on top and even it out with a fork, to make nice indentations that will go golden and crunchy. Dot with extra butter if you like.

⑥ Preheat grill or oven to 220°C/gas mark 7 and transfer the dish to crisp up the potato topping. This dish keeps well in the fridge for 3 days or so and the flavour improves. Reheat by baking in an oven at 180°C/gas mark 4 for 35 minutes.

CHAPS'S BROAD BEAN AND
SMOKED TROUT SALAD

S alad? Isn't that for vegetarians, people on diets and other wimps of this world? Well, yes, but there are those rare sunny days in Blighty when a bowl of hot soup just isn't the ticket, whether you are entertaining or not. Anyway, this isn't one of those irritatingly crispy Continental salads, with floppy lettuce leaves spraying olive oil everywhere, where you are lucky to find the odd prawn or anything with a bit of flavour. Our salad is 100% body, flavour and manly vigour.

♦ INGREDIENTS ♦

Serves 2

2 hot-smoked trout fillets
150g frozen broad beans, defrosted and slipped from their skins so just the emerald beans remain
3 sprigs of dill, snipped
tiny pinch mace
salt and freshly ground black pepper

For lemon butter dressing
40g unsalted butter
juice of ¼ lemon

(or)

For lemon vinaigrette dressing
3 tablespoons oil
2 teaspoons cider vinegar
1 teaspoon lemon juice
a pinch of sugar

(1) On a hot day, serve this dish chilled from the fridge with the vinaigrette dressing. If it's one of the other 363 days of the British year, take the ingredients out of the fridge an hour before using, so you can serve them at room temperature and dress with the lemon butter dressing. The flavour will be better.

(2) Break the trout fillets into large pieces, drop into a large bowl and add the defrosted beans, snipped dill, mace and seasoning. Gently turn it over with your hands to mix and blend the flavours.

(3) To make the lemon butter dressing: gently melt the butter in a saucepan and add the lemon. The mixture should be just warm, not hot. To make the vinaigrette dressing: simply whisk the ingredients together in a jug.

(4) Carefully spoon the salad ingredients on to plates or a serving dish and drizzle with your chosen dressing.

Broad beans are very good frozen and this is a useful standby dish, as you are likely, if you have followed the advice in our stores section at the beginning of the book, to have most of the ingredients to hand.

BAKED TROUT
WITH LOVAGE & BACON

Serious fishermen love the challenge of catching trout as they are thrashy little blighters that resist the hook with all their might. If you live anywhere near a freshwater lake, you may be able to purchase a trout or twain from one of the green-clad fellows lurking on the shore; if not, trout is available everywhere – try to ensure it's brown trout as opposed to rainbow or golden, as the former is far tastier. The fish are rather bony but worth it – keep a loaf of bread handy to pass to anyone who swallows a bone.

EQUIPMENT

Cocktail sticks or skewers

♦ INGREDIENTS ♦

Serves 4

4 whole (preferably brown) trout, gutted
juice of ½ lemon
a handful of lovage, chopped
150g butter
8 slices of smoked streaky bacon
sprinkle of salt and freshly ground black pepper

(1) Preheat oven to 200°C/gas mark 6.

(2) Rinse and dry the trout. Chop off the heads and tails, if you prefer – or ask your fishmonger to do it for you. You could also ask your fishmonger to fillet them.

(3) Season the insides with a sprinkle of salt and pepper, a squeeze of lemon and the chopped lovage and pieces of butter, saving a little butter to rub over the fish skin.

(4) Stretch the rashers of bacon using the back of your knife and wrap two around each trout. Secure with a cocktail stick or skewer and bung on to a baking dish or roasting tin.

(5) Bake in the oven for 15 minutes and serve immediately.

SALSIFY, SCALLOPS AND FIZZ

Salsify is called the oyster of vegetables and perhaps for this reason is difficult to find. Should you be one of those chaps with a kitchen garden, you might want to have a stab at growing the stuff. If you can't be bothered, we have offered you the alternative of using Jerusalem artichokes, which, despite looking like gnarled old witches' hands, are delicious. We've recommended using Breaky Bottom fizz, which we rate as a particularly good example of a newish British champagne, but you can use any white wine you like.

◆ INGREDIENTS ◆

Serves 4

a handful of salsify, cut into
   3cm pieces, or Jerusalem
   artichokes – either veg
   needs to be peeled and kept
   in water with a drop of
   vinegar until needed or they
   will turn brown
150ml Breaky Bottom sparkling
   wine
150ml fish stock
16 scallops – big ones – off
   the shells but wash and keep
   the shells if you can
40g butter
salt and freshly ground black
   pepper
75ml whipping or double
   cream, whipped to soft
   peaks, to serve (optional)

1. Put the salsify or artichokes with the wine and fish stock in a wide saucepan. Bring to the boil, then simmer for approx. 10–12 minutes until the veg are nearly tender when pierced with a knife.

2. Drop the scallops into the pan to poach in the liquor for a couple of minutes, turning them over.

3. Using a slotted spoon, take the veg and scallops out of the liquor and arrange on a warm serving dish, or spoon back into the shells. Turn up the heat, reduce the sauce by half, and then whisk in a little butter. Spoon over the scallops and veg and serve with a dollop of whipped cream on each shell if desired.

OYSTER LOAVES

According to Jane Grigson, this is one of the best British eighteenth-century dishes ever. Oyster loaves have been around since first being recorded in *English Housewifry* by Elizabeth Moxon in 1764. They stuck around for at least a century as a staple of the upper crust, Benjamin Disraeli's play *Venetia* giving them a mention: 'The repast closed with a dish of oyster loaves and a pompetone of larks.' If it all sounds like a line from 'The Twelve Days of Christmas', then that should be reason enough to foist these delicious parcels of flavour on to your guests.

EQUIPMENT

Pastry brush for brushing melted butter (or you can use a teaspoon and fingers)

♦ I N G R E D I E N T S ♦

Serves 2

2 part-baked rolls
50g unsalted butter, melted in a saucepan
4 large oysters, shucked, liquor reserved
pinch of cayenne pepper or couple of drops of Tabasco sauce
4 tablespoons double or clotted cream
squeeze of lemon juice
salt and freshly ground pepper

① Preheat oven to 220°C/gas mark 7.

② Cut the tops off the rolls and scoop out the interior crumb, being careful not to pierce the walls. Brush inside and out with some of the melted butter – don't forget the lids.

③ Bake for 10 minutes until crisp and golden – keep an eye on them so they don't burn.

④ Drop the oysters into the saucepan containing the remainder of the melted butter and cook gently until opaque – 1–2 minutes. Take them out and cut them in half.

⑤ Into the saucepan with the oystery butter goes the strained liquor, cayenne or Tabasco, cream, lemon and salt and pepper. Boil this sauce until it becomes lovely and thick. Use a whisk to stop it separating. If you are cooking ahead, you can stop at this point and chill everything.

⑥ When ready to serve, gently reheat the sauce and then drop in the oysters to warm through. Spoon into the rolls, replace their lids and serve immediately.

GAME OLD BIRD

A stew that can, in a flash, become a pie, depending on how much trouble you wish to take. The season will decide what game you can use, and your skill with a shotgun whether you should bag it yourself or buy it in a supermarket. This recipe will give you a good start in the art of building flavour gradually, combining sweet and salty additions. The result is an unctuous blend of flavours that will have your guests wondering how you created such a 'gamey' stew.

EQUIPMENT

Large casserole dish with
    well-fitting lid

♦ INGREDIENTS ♦

Serves 4–6

approx. 800g game meat
    (pigeon, rabbit, pheasant,
    venison, etc.), cut into largish
    pieces
2 tablespoons goose fat
3 slices of streaky bacon, chopped
1 tablespoon flour
1 tablespoon wine vinegar
250ml port or 200ml red wine plus
    50ml sherry or brandy
500ml game or chicken stock
1 teaspoon anchovy paste
10 shallots
2 apples, peeled, cored and
    roughly chopped
1 small celeriac or turnip, peeled
    and diced into 3cm chunks
approx. 20 button mushrooms
    or 5 field mushrooms, sliced
2 tablespoons honey or brown
    sugar
4 crushed juniper berries
½ teaspoon mixed spice
3 tablespoons pink peppercorns
sprig of rosemary, thyme or
    lovage, if you have some handy
freshly ground black pepper and
    just a pinch of salt

If turning into a pie:
1 sheet ready-rolled puff pastry
1 egg, beaten, for brushing – or a
    little milk
flat-leaf parsley or lovage, roughly
    chopped (optional)

① If using the oven, preheat to 170°C/gas mark 3. Take the meat out of fridge (it is always a good idea to cook meat from room temperature) and season the meat lightly with salt and pepper while it sits to come up to temperature.

② Melt the goose fat in a casserole dish and add the bacon. Stir around until golden.

③ Now add the meat, stir around, add the flour and stir until mixed in. Pour on the vinegar and port or red wine and sherry/brandy mixture, let it bubble up and give the bottom a good scrape to deglaze the pan.

④ Stir in the stock and anchovy paste and then add the shallots, apples, celeriac or turnip, mushrooms, honey or sugar, juniper berries, mixed spice, pink peppercorns, black pepper and a sprig of rosemary, thyme or lovage, if using.

⑤ Put a lid on the casserole dish and either simmer very gently on the hob or bake in the oven for 1½ hours. Give it a good stir and check for seasoning before serving.

If turning into a pie
① Simply cut out 4–6 jolly shapes from a sheet of puff pastry. Take your stew out of the oven and turn up the temperature to 200°C/gas mark 6. Lay the puff pastry on a baking tray, brush with beaten egg or milk and bake for 7–10 minutes until golden.

② To serve, bring the stew to the table with the puff pastry shapes neatly arranged on top. You can also sprinkle over a good handful of roughly chopped flat-leaf parsley or lovage.

REAL CHAP'S SALAD
STEAK WITH ANCHOVIES & TRUFFLE OIL

✕

Our other salad, of only two (see page 43), is similarly devoid of anything too 'salady'. The only compensation for eating salad is the pleasant surprise of finding interesting, weighty, salty, tasty ingredients among all the green stuff, and this salad delivers on all such fronts. The seemingly odd bedfellows of beef and anchovies were once used together much more frequently, partly because one always would have a can or two of anchovies knocking about the store cupboard (as you should). Like our other salad, there is no lettuce – in our view a vegetable that benefits much more from being braised (see page 118) rather than filling up a salad bowl with its boring greenness.

EQUIPMENT

Large freezer bag

◆ INGREDIENTS ◆

Serves 6–8

1kg beef skirt (trimmed weight)
6 anchovies
4 tablespoons truffle oil (or you can use rapeseed or sunflower oil)
1 teaspoon crushed black peppercorns

For the salad
3 bunches watercress
3 bunches radishes – hot ones
a little oil
squeeze of lemon
salt and freshly ground black pepper

① Put the piece of beef into a large freezer bag and massage the anchovies, oil and peppercorns into the beef. Seal and allow to marinate at room temperature for 3 hours, or transfer the bag to the fridge and leave the beef in the marinade for up to 24 hours.

② When ready to serve, preheat the grill to very hot. Take the beef out of the bag, place under the grill and cook quickly – a couple of minutes on either side. Remove the beef from the grill and allow to rest for 10 minutes before cutting into strips or slices.

③ Meanwhile, prepare the salad. Wash and pick over the watercress, removing most tough stalks. Slice the radishes as thinly as you like or are able to. Just before serving, put into a bowl and drizzle over oil, a squeeze of lemon and a little salt and pepper. Stir well to coat every leaf and slice.

④ Arrange on a plate. Top with strips of the hot beef and serve immediately.

ARABELLA'S BANGERS
IN WHITE WINE

Arabella Boxer was known – and still is, in certain Kensington circles – for recipes that adapted French bourgeois cookery for the upper middle-class English dinner table, so you would find things like clear duck soup or *oeufs en gelée* adorning the tables of our own haute bourgeoisie during the 1970s. Boxer's approach is worthy of posterity and we have picked this less fanciful recipe purely because it is less French than many of her others. It is also a very good, warming dish to serve on a blustery winter's day, perhaps after a long walk.

♦ I N G R E D I E N T S ♦

Serves 4

12 very good-quality, fat
    pork sausages
50g butter
2 large onions, sliced into
    rings
1 fresh bay leaf
6 ripe tomatoes
1 tablespoon flour
300ml white wine
salt and freshly ground
    black pepper

(1) Warm a large frying pan over a medium heat. Put in the (unpricked) sausages to brown – there's no need to add any fat as they'll soon provide their own. Add the butter, onions and bay leaf and gently sweat the onions until soft, buttery and translucent.

(2) Meanwhile, skin the tomatoes. The quickest method is not the water method, which is rather messy. Instead, quarter the tomato, scrape out and discard the seeds. Pressing the tomato flat, skin-side down, take a sharp knife and cut horizontally into the flesh, pressing down against the board as you go. This removes the skin easily and does not waste the flesh. It is a skill worth learning, as tomatoes do taste sweeter and better without skin and seeds – and look lovely in salads. Roughly chop the tomato pieces.

(3) When the onions are nice and soft, add the tomatoes and cook for a couple of minutes. Add the flour and stir about for a further couple of minutes.

(4) Pour over the wine and 100ml water, stirring well to stop any lumps forming. Season and then allow to bubble away for about 20 minutes before serving. This dish reheats easily and well. It keeps for a couple of days in the fridge and freezes for up to 3 months.

ROSE VEAL
IN BREADCRUMBS

Although there is something rather *Fawlty Towers* about an escalope, there is also something of the old-fashioned gentlemen's club about it. Done well, a veal escalope can be just the thing to offer for lunch to guests who are not ravenously hungry, yet neither in the mood for a sandwich (which you would never offer to your guests, unless you were serving afternoon tea, and even then only cucumber ones). We are going to show how to do one well. For those still anti-veal, you should know that we now have rose veal (used here), which is kindly raised – no more veal crates.

◆ INGREDIENTS ◆

Serves 4

4 rose veal escalopes
3 tablespoons milk
3 tablespoons flour
1 egg, beaten
80g breadcrumbs
1 tablespoon goose
    fat
50g butter
plenty of salt and freshly
    ground black pepper
lemon wedges or your
    favourite sauce, to serve

(1) Put the escalopes between two sheets of baking parchment, or in a freezer bag, and pound with a rolling pin until they are only a couple of millimetres thick. Sprinkle with salt and pepper on both sides. Set aside to allow them to come up to room temperature.

(2) Have the milk, flour, egg and breadcrumbs lined up in separate shallow dishes and dip the escalopes one by one in each dish, creating a nice even coating of each.

(3) Heat the goose fat and butter in a frying pan until nicely hot, lay in the escalopes and fry until crisp and golden. Turn over and fry the other side until crisp and golden. Serve immediately or keep warm in the oven for 10 minutes or so before serving, while you get the vegetables ready (see Chapter 6 for ideas).

(4) Serve with wedges of lemon or with your favourite sauce.

24-HOUR GLAZED
ROAST PORK BELLY
IN CIDER

In some countries, spending a couple of days cooking a great feast for the whole village is something that casually happens every couple of weeks. In this country, we baulk at spending more than half an hour in the kitchen to prepare lunch or dinner, believing that there are 'more important' things to do – like watching television or looking at things to buy on the Internet. This prime piece of pork gets to spend a full 24 hours in the oven, lucky old thing – but guess what? The amount of time we need you actually to be in the kitchen yourself amounts to a paltry 20 minutes or so!

EQUIPMENT

Large ovenproof dish or
    roasting tin

♦ INGREDIENTS ♦

Serves 10–12 (good for leftovers)

2kg pork belly – use free-
    range good stuff
1 teaspoon caraway seeds
1 teaspoon mustard seeds
scraping of nutmeg
500ml cider
450g cored apples – any sort:
    large Bramleys or even eating
    apples
salt and freshly ground black
    pepper

For the glaze
2 tablespoons honey
2 tablespoons brown sugar
2 tablespoons salt

① Put the pork into a large dish that will fit in the oven and rub it all over with the spices and some salt and pepper. Pour around the cider. Cover with a layer of baking parchment and then a layer of foil, sealed well around the edges.

② Put the whole lot into the oven and bake at 100°C/gas mark ¼ for 23 hours. Check from time to time and baste the meat.

③ You can bake the apples whole, if you have a separate oven, at 190°C/gas mark 5 for approx. 30–40 minutes. Alternatively, an hour before serving, add the apples to the dish with the pork and return to the oven to cook through.

④ Twenty minutes before serving, take the pork out of the oven. Turn up the temperature to 220°C/gas mark 7. Drain off and reserve the juices. Pat the pork dry with kitchen paper and paint it with honey, brown sugar and salt. Return it to the dish and put back in the oven to colour and crisp for 10–15 minutes.

⑤ Let the juices stand for a few minutes and tip off any fat that collects at the top. Taste the juices – they should be delicious. Reheat in the microwave or a small pan until piping hot. Serve in a jug alongside the pork, which should be brought to the table on a beautiful dish surrounded by the apples. The meat will be so soft that you can serve it with a spoon.

CHRISTMAS LUNCH

There is no need for Christmas lunch to have the unsurprising monotony of school dinners. Why not personalise the meal, while retaining its agreeable sense of occasion and grandeur? Our two recipes are at opposite ends of the gastronomic scale, from the nobly ascetic to the regally opulent.

◆ ROAST BEEF WITH CLARET ◆

Digby Anderson was one of the great inspirations for this book. An irascible, grumpy food critic for *The Spectator* in the 1980s, most of his rants against the mediocrity of British food were entirely justifiable. In *The English at Table*, he lamented the way we keep virtually nothing in our store cupboards, yet go and spend a fortune on all the ingredients for a dinner party. As a nation, we are particularly good at squandering money on fripperies used only once at Christmas. Digby's recommended Christmas lunch involved the purchase of just one decent joint of beef, served with a glass of claret and nothing else whatsoever. Sublime. *Pictured on pages 60–61.*

EQUIPMENT

A meat thermometer

◆ INGREDIENTS ◆

Serves about 12

2kg fine piece of very good, well hung, beef fillet (for Digby Anderson purists – choose one of even girth for even cooking) or 3kg beef rib, which looks splendidly theatrical (see photograph)
50g beef dripping, for rubbing
a few carrots, halved onions and celery sticks
bottle of Claret (half for cooking and the rest to serve)
plenty of salt and freshly ground black pepper

 ① Make a note of the weight of the beef: critical for correct cooking. At some point a day or two before, rub your fillet with beef dripping and salt and pepper. Arrange the carrots, onions and celery to create a trivet in a roasting tin. Place the beef on top. Cover to keep it hygienic and refrigerate.

② A few hours before cooking, get the roasting tin out of the fridge so you can ensure your beef goes into the oven at room temperature.

③ Preheat oven to 220°C/gas mark 7.

④ Pour about ½ bottle of Claret into the roasting tin, avoiding the meat. This will make your gravy afterwards. Plunge the beef on its vegetable trivet into the oven for 10 minutes, turn down the heat to 200°C/gas mark 6 and cook for 15 minutes per kilogram. This will ensure a pink centre. When it's ready, a meat thermometer stuck into the centre should read 55°C.

⑤ Take the meat out of the oven. Transfer it to a warm serving dish. Let it rest, well covered (I use a layer of foil and then a few tea-towels piled on top) in a warm place, for 15 minutes. Strain the juices from the pan into a jug and check the seasoning. Serve with a glass of Claret.

SLOW-ROAST GOOSE WITH APPLES AND CHESTNUTS

This elegant, slow method of roasting ensures both succulent, flavourful meat and a hassle-free Christmas day. You put the bird in the oven 6 hours ahead of lunchtime, and allow 20 minutes for it to rest. It's better not to stuff goose because it absorbs so much of the fat. If you insist on serving stuffing, make it into balls to serve around the bird or in a separate dish.

EQUIPMENT

Large roasting tin and metal
   trivet

♦ I N G R E D I E N T S ♦

Serves 10

4.5kg goose – giblet bag
   removed
sea salt and freshly ground
   black pepper
bunch of sage, flat-leaf parsley
   or bay leaves, to garnish

To fill the cavity:
1 orange, whole
1 lemon, whole
2 shallots, whole
2 fresh bay leaves
8 sprigs of thyme
small bunch of fresh flat-leaf
   parsley

For the gravy
50ml brandy
250–300ml white wine
400ml good chicken stock
2 teaspoons cornflour mixed
   with 2 teaspoons water (to
   thicken, if you must)

For the apples and chestnuts:
50g butter
50g brown sugar
6 apples, quartered and cored
200g peeled chestnuts (vacuum-
   packed are easiest) roughly,
   chopped (reserve a few whole
   for garnish)
juice of 1 orange

① 1–2 hours before cooking, get goosey out of the fridge, remove the giblets and wipe out the cavity with kitchen paper. Massage all over with 3 teaspoons sea salt and lots of black pepper, sprinkling a little inside the cavity too. Then pop in all the cavity ingredients – their flavours will infuse the bird nicely. Allow it to sit for 1–2 hours to come up to room temperature.

② Preheat your oven to 140°C/gas mark 1. Sit the bird on a metal trivet in the roasting tin and cook for 6 hours, spooning over the aromatic juices a couple of times.

③ After 5 hours, collect the juices from the roasting tin and stand them in a cool place to separate, then remove the fat layer that forms on the surface. Reserve the juices to add to the gravy. Pierce the thickest part of the goose's thigh with a skewer after 5½ hours to see if the juices run clear – if so, it is done. If not, cook on for the full 6 hours.

④ Once your goose is cooked, take it out of the oven and cover in foil and tea towels to keep it hot while it relaxes for 20 minutes. This allows the juices to be retained in the meat and makes for better carving.

⑤ For the apples and chestnuts, melt the butter in a large, heavy-based frying pan and add the sugar. Stir to melt over a low to medium heat. Add the apples; you will have to stand them on end. Stud them in between with chestnuts. The apples will soften and collapse slightly as they cook. After 10 minutes, pour over the orange juice and let it bubble away for 5 minutes, then spoon this delicious concoction around the bird.

⑥ To make the gravy, put the goose roasting tin on the hob over a medium to high heat. Deglaze the pan by pouring in the brandy – stand back as it will flame for a second – then the wine and chicken stock, plus the reserved juices. Stir, scrape and bubble for a few minutes, adding the cornflour mix if you wish. Taste for seasoning. Pour into a warmed jug.

⑦ When all is ready, transfer the goose onto a warmed, splendid plate, spoon around the apples and chestnuts and decorate with your chosen bunches of herb. This dish is perfect served by candlelight, which shouldn't be difficult as it's usually dark by lunchtime on Christmas Day.

CHAPTER 3

AFTERNOON TEA

Afternoon tea is one of those meals that distinguishes us from savage animals. Other creatures may take breakfast, lunch and dinner, but you don't see many hyenas pouring loose leaf teas into dainty china cups and saucers at 4pm. The very pointlessness of afternoon tea is its precise joy, and if it spoils your appetite for dinner, just skip dinner and go straight to supper.

A note on etiquette:

Hosts: Serve tea from a pot, via a tea strainer. Don't use teabags unless you are actually a student. Avoid using the phrase 'Shall I be mother?' altogether and just pour the tea if you are the host/ess. Add the milk after the tea (see page 69 for why this is the correct procedure). Stir the tea from side to side as opposed to in a circular motion; do not let the teaspoon rattle on the sides of the cup.

Guests: Hold the saucer roughly at chest height and sip the tea, holding the cup's handle between your fingers, not with one hooked through it. Ensure that your little finger is safely tucked away, unless you want to appear terribly nouveau riche. Avoid uttering 'Ahhh!' having drained your cup, however good the tea was. If impressed, simply ask your host what blend they used. Wait for your host to offer a refill rather than helping yourself.

POTTED TROUT

We've all heard of potted shrimp and they are still being devoured at the Reform Club as we speak, but this recipe takes a more substantial brain food – much favoured by Jeeves, incidentally – and shoves it into a pot, for ease of scooping out and spreading on toast or English muffins. It's a tasty, zingy paste that can revive flagging spirits after an exhausting game of croquet, or it can be the centrepiece of a light picnic. Trout is at such an extreme end of the savoury spectrum that it balances well with the sort of sweet foods one would expect at a summer picnic or a garden tea party.

EQUIPMENT

Something to pot the trout into, e.g. glass tumbler, old teacup or similar vessel

♦ INGREDIENTS ♦

Serves 4

1 fillet hot-smoked trout
—the pale pink stuff, not the ersatz smoked salmon stuff
100ml single cream
tiny pinch of mace
tiny pinch of white pepper
1 teaspoon finely chopped dill or chervil or even tarragon or lovage (optional)
sprig of some pretty herb or edible flower from the garden, e.g. nasturtiums or violets, to garnish

For the clarified butter (optional)
100g unsalted butter

① Put the smoked trout in a large bowl, pour in the cream and add the mace and white pepper. Mash with a potato masher or a fork until well mashed. Using a large spoon or spatula, give it all a thorough stir to bring it together.

② If you like, fold some finely chopped dill or chervil (or tarragon or lovage) through the mixture.

③ Pile it into a little pot, ramekin, jar, etc. and whack the bottom sharply on a work surface to release any air bubbles. Now smooth the surface and, if using a flower or sprig of herb, place it on top.

④ To make clarified butter (you can skip this step but it does give a nice finish): melt the butter in a small saucepan. Once melted you will see the clear golden butter, and on the bottom, the milky whey residue. Pour off the golden melted butter, taking care to leave the milky deposits behind (these spoil faster and affect the keeping quality). Pour or spoon your clarified butter directly onto the surface of the potted trout: you can keep any surplus in the fridge for another use – it is very good for frying things as it doesn't burn easily.

⑤ Chill the pot in the fridge for the butter to set.

If taking this on a picnic, it will travel well in a cool box. At the tea table it will spread nicely on hot buttered crumpets, muffins or toast.

QUAILS' EGGS

Quails' eggs are fun for all the family: their pulchritude has the adults reaching for their watercolour sets, and their cutesy size appeals to children. Since they taste virtually the same as hen's eggs, no one is in for a shock. They are a bit of a fiddle to peel, so help your guests out by peeling most of them in advance and just leaving a few unpeeled ones when you serve. The traditional accompaniment to quails' eggs is celery salt but some may find that rather strong, so offer good-quality sea salt as an alternative.

To cook quails' eggs – plunge into boiling water and cook for the following times:

Hard-boiled – 4 minutes
Soft-boiled – 2½ minutes

To stop dark rings appearing on the eggs, drain immediately and run the cold tap on them constantly for 5 minutes until they are cold. This will also help them peel very easily.

CUCUMBER SANDWICHES

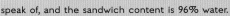

The insubstantiality of a cucumber sandwich is its *raison d'être*. Created so that Victorian gentlemen could scoff something at teatime without spoiling their dinner, the removal of the crusts ensures they have virtually no calories to speak of, and the sandwich content is 96% water.

Even so, they are surprisingly difficult to get right, and wrongly constructed can end up being a damp, unwanted pile on the tea table. The secret is to remove the soggy part before they even reach the plate, by peeling the cucumber, carefully cutting it lengthways and coring out the pips in the middle, then slicing it with a cheese grater rather than a knife. The salting process also draws out further moisture as well as flavour – 20 minutes is adequate for this.

STICKY GINGER CAKE

This is a classic English cake, but one that requires no eggs, so you can knock one up whenever you feel like it without resorting to a shopping expedition. It uses the melting method, which carries no risk of curdling: it's fast, easy and not at all messy. This ginger cake has great keeping qualities; you can bring it out of hiding up to two weeks after you make it, and it will taste all the better for it. What a perfect gift, too, to take to a house party; a spicy ginger cake will be much more effusively received than boring old chocolate any day. It also makes a superb pudding, warmed up or at room temperature with custard, or with clotted cream at tea time.

EQUIPMENT

Cake tin approx. 20cm
  diameter

◆ INGREDIENTS ◆

*Serves 8, depending on greed/
generosity of slices*

175g plain flour
110g soft brown sugar
2 tablespoons ground
  ginger
175g black treacle
30g butter
½ teaspoon bicarbonate
  of soda

① Preheat oven to 175°C/gas mark 3. Line the cake tin with baking parchment – cut two long strips and just overlap them. Allow extra to hang over the sides so you can use it to lift the cake out of the tin.

② Mix the flour, sugar and ginger together in a large mixing bowl. In a small bowl, mix the treacle, butter, bicarb and 125ml boiling water. Add this to the dry mixture and stir until smooth.

③ Pour the whole lot into the prepared tin and bake for 30–40 minutes. Test by inserting a skewer or sharp implement into the centre and seeing if it comes out clean, not covered in cake batter.

④ Remove from the oven. Cover the tin with a clean tea-towel for 5 minutes or so, before turning out the cake onto a cooling rack. If you don't have a cooling rack, a grilling rack will work just as well. Peel off the paper and allow to cool. Once the cake is cool, put it into a cake tin and leave for a couple of days for the flavour and squidginess to develop – if you can wait that long.

BOILED FRUIT CAKE

Worry not, this cake isn't actually boiled – the fruit is, which produces a moist, lovely flavoured cake. This recipe came from the grandmother of Denise Bagnall-Oakeley, one of the great inspirations for this book, and has been in the family for generations. If you don't have a cake tin, either because the former Mrs Chap took it with her when she went to stay with her mother, or you simply don't know where they sell them, use an old cake or biscuit tin to bake the fruit cake in. As long as you properly grease it, once the finished cake pops out, you don't have to transfer it anywhere – just keep it in the tin until it's finished.

EQUIPMENT

Square baking tin approx.
    22cm diameter or an
    old-fashioned biscuit tin

◆ INGREDIENTS ◆

*Serves 8, depending on greed/
generosity of slices*

110g unsalted butter
110g soft brown sugar
1 tablespoon golden syrup
    or treacle
400g mixed vine fruit
(sultanas, raisins, etc.) with
    mixed peel – you need a
    ratio of 50g mixed peel to
    350g dried fruit
225g self-raising flour
¼ teaspoon salt
1 egg, beaten
1 teaspoon almond or
    vanilla extract
1 teaspoon bicarbonate
    of soda mixed with
    1 tablespoon warm
    milk
2 tablespoons Demerara
    sugar to dredge on top

① Preheat oven to 175°C/gas mark 3.

② Put the butter, sugar, syrup or treacle, fruit, peel and 175ml water in a large saucepan. Bring slowly to the boil, reduce the heat, cover with a lid (or baking sheet) and simmer gently for 15 minutes.

③ Meanwhile line your square tin with baking parchment – cut two long strips and just overlap them. Allow extra to hang over the sides so you can use it to lift the cake out of the tin. The cake will also keep well in the tin.

④ Take the saucepan off the heat and stir to cool a little. Gently fold in the flour and salt, not worrying if you can still see some bits of flour; over stirring will make for a heavy cake. Now add the egg, almond or vanilla extract and the warm milk mixture. Gently mix again until combined.

⑤ Pour the mixture into the prepared tin. For a pretty, crunchy topping, sprinkle the surface with a couple of tablespoons of sugar. Smooth the top and tap the tin gently to release any air bubbles. As long as you line the tin with baking parchment and not greaseproof paper, the cake will come out perfectly.

⑥ Plonk the tin into the centre of the oven and bake for 45 minutes until nicely golden. Check for doneness by inserting the blade of a sharp knife into the centre and making sure it comes out clean. Remove from the oven and let stand for a few minutes to gather its wits. Then turn out onto a cooling rack, peel away the paper and let it cool completely. This will keep in a cake tin for approx. 1 week.

CINNAMON TOAST

Alright, you've got your scones, some dainty cucumber sandwiches and a cake or two, all waiting for your guests on a lovely Victorian cake stand while the kettle boils. But wait a minute, isn't there something missing? What if one of your guests doesn't like scones? Sounds unbelievable, but some people find scones too heavy and too sweet, with all the jam and cream. So, for those fusspots who want gradually to ease their way from cucumber sandwich to fruit cake, cinnamon toast comes as the perfect interlude.

◆ I N G R E D I E N T S ◆

Serves 2

50g butter, softened at room temperature
50g sugar – Demerara is fun for crunch but you can use soft brown or caster
1 teaspoon cinnamon
4 slices white bread

(1) Put the butter, sugar and cinnamon in a mixing bowl - beat until smooth and well mixed.

(2) Toast the bread.

(3) Spread the toast generously with the cinnamon butter right up to and including the crusts.

(4) Put under the grill to warm and bubble and caramelise – but not burn! Watch it like a hawk and whip out at the first sign of cremation.

(5) Cut into pieces and serve.

THE MILK/TEA IN FIRST DEBATE

The order of service *vis-à-vis* tea and milk has been rattling teacups for centuries and there are various theories as to whether the tea or the milk should go into the cup first. The most plausible is that Below Stairs the staff had earthenware mugs of poor quality, so they put the milk in first to avoid the mugs cracking. Meanwhile, Upstairs, the cups were made from bone china and porcelain and consequently more durable, so the tea was poured in first. If the cup cracked, it was simply chucked away and someone was sent out to buy another set. So base your decision on which order to pour the tea and milk on whether you can afford to replace any broken crockery. Just don't use mugs when serving afternoon tea, please.

A SINGULAR SCONE

Afternoon tea would not be complete without some hot, fresh scones, but everyone dreads the mess they can make of the kitchen. Our method avoids all that hassle and allows you to stroll into the kitchen, spend a few happy moments there, put the kettle on and await your perfect scones. For a start, forget about fiddling about with cutters: just make one huge circle with all the dough and score it into wedges. Then, when they are baked, you can easily snap off each triangular, perfect scone. That way you are only handling a single item on the baking tray, rather than dozens of little items that can easily be dropped or broken. You simply lift the scored circular scone on to the cooling rack in one swift movement and cut into individual scones when cooled. The actual scone-making process should be fast, with minimal handling. If you have a food-processor, use it. If not, a nice big bowl will do nicely.

EQUIPMENT

Food-processor (optional)
A cooling rack
– not essential but the
    bottom can go soggy
Pastry brush – or you can
    use kitchen paper or your
    hands

♦ INGREDIENTS ♦

Serves 2 hungry people

225g self-raising flour
¼ teaspoon salt
50g unsalted butter,
    softened
150ml milk plus a squeeze
    of lemon or ½ teaspoon
    vinegar
a little extra milk, to glaze
    (optional)
jam and clotted cream, to
    serve

① Preheat oven 200°C/gas mark 6. Line a baking tray with baking parchment and lightly flour the surface.

② Tip the flour and salt into a bowl and stir to combine. Add the butter. Rub and squeeze the ingredients together until they resemble breadcrumbs. Don't spend too long on it – a few rough bits are good.

③ Make a well in the middle and pour in the milk and lemon/vinegar mixture. Using a butter knife, stir and cut the mixture until just mixed. Use your hands to knead it a couple of times, wiping the dough around the sides of the bowl to gather all the leftover bits. The dough should be soft and slightly sticky. If it's dry, add a sprinkle more milk to help it.

④ Lift out the dough and dump it onto the lightly floured baking parchment on your baking tray. Using your hands, gently bring it together in a circle about 10cm wide and 4cm thick.

⑤ Now, using a large knife dipped in flour, score the surface into 4 wedges. For a shiny top, quickly brush just the surface with a little milk.

⑥ Whack it in the oven for 20–30 minutes or until risen and lightly golden. Remove and place on a cooling rack – cover with a tea-towel if you like soft crusts. Serve warm if you can. Guests can split and fill their own scones. Serve with jam spooned on first, then clotted cream for the Cornish cream tea; cream first, then jam for the Devonshire cream tea.

HIGH TEA DRINKS

LAND OF MILK AND HONEY

Warm some milk and stir in a teaspoon of good-quality honey – set honey is better than runny. This is rather restorative when you are feeling under the weather, and the addition of whisky further elevates the healing properties.

HOT CHOCOLATE

Measure out a mugful of milk, tip into a saucepan, add a few squares of dark chocolate, and then stir with a little whisk until it nearly comes to the boil.

MADEIRA

Madeira was popularised by the comedy duo Flanders & Swann in the 1950s, since when few Englishmen are able to serve it to a lady without saying, 'Have some Madeira, my dear.' However, serving it without saying this phrase will mark you down as a true eccentric, so the choice is yours. The main thing is not to serve anything other than fortified wine of some sort as an aperitif. Gin and tonic smacks of expats on Mallorca in 1974.

PIMM'S

A jolly good chap, James Pimm, first produced Pimm's in 1823. Winter Cup is based on brandy, unlike its better-known variant, Pimm's No. 1 Cup, which is based on gin. Mix one-part Pimm's Winter Cup with three-parts warm apple juice; add slices of apple and orange, and serve in a teacup – for that Prohibition feel – or in a tumbler, for that Permissive Society feel.

Other suitable beverage offerings with High Tea are sherry and its variants, such as Manzanilla, Amontillado and Oloroso. Cream sherry should exclusively be offered to female family members aged 75 or over.

— CHAPTER 4 —

HIGH TEA & PICNICS

High tea is a lost tradition ripe for reintroduction. The setting should be a large table perfectly groaning with food. Guests can stand, sit on sofas or whatever they like. Everything in the feast is already prepared and served either hot or cold but ready for guests to help themselves. High tea is perfect for birthdays, entertaining aunts and generally for people you don't want to hang around for too long. The idea is that you give them a good feed, but they are not stuck at your table for ages, waiting for their after-dinner mint until the wee hours. In the old days, high tea for the farming classes was the main meal of the evening, taken at about 5pm. They may have had a snack before bed or just a milky drink. Today we can think of high tea as an excuse to have all our favourite things on a table; not worrying about having sweet things before savoury and letting everyone choose what order they eat in. The meal is also incredibly useful if heading off to take in some weighty cultural event early in the evening; high tea will keep you going until suppertime.

PICNIC ETIQUETTE

Incredible as it may seem, the Victorians managed to get through entire picnics with only two or three servants. Today we are expected to survive them without any staff at all, which is why all the food preparation should be done at home, ready to be unpacked and served upon arrival. When you arrive, choose your site carefully: perched on the edge of a cliff may be picturesque, but always allow for that one chap who takes too readily to the Pimm's putting a damper on the whole afternoon by pitching off the cliff. Not too sunny a spot either – you don't really expect ladies to hold their parasols while dining, do you? In the absence of servants, gentlemen are expected to do the manly stuff like opening tight Tupperware boxes and shaking the vinaigrette. Finally, let's leave it to the Victorians to advise on seating arrangements: 'If a woman chooses to seat herself upon the ground, a gentleman is not at liberty to follow her example unless he has been invited to do so.'

GAME TERRINE

Game terrine, like revenge, is a dish best served cold, although if you wish, you may serve it warm as well – the terrine, that is. Hilda Leyel was a well-known herbalist of the 1920s, founding the Society of Herbalists in 1927 (now the Herb Society, still going strong today). Leyel also wrote cookery books and this recipe comes from her *Gentle Art of Cookery*. It is surprisingly short on herbs but very rich in game, which, compressed into a tight space and drowned in consommé, makes for a spectacularly meaty dish guaranteed to liven up any picnic. This is a surprisingly low-fat dish for something so meaty.

EQUIPMENT

Hilda stipulates a glass soufflé dish, but any pretty oven proof dish will do in the right size for your quantities. A 1-litre dish is the minimum.

♦ INGREDIENTS ♦

Serves 4-6

400g game, boned and trimmed: rabbit, pheasant, venison – cut into 5cm pieces
a generous pinch each of cracked black pepper, cayenne pepper and salt
400g can consommé – must be good quality – should be jellied when you open it or it will not set
2 tablespoons sherry or brandy (optional)
fresh flat-leaf parsley, to serve

Hilda describes the method thus: 'Put some raw joints of boned game into a glass soufflé dish and season very heavily with black pepper, cayenne and salt. Fill up the dish with consommé and bake in the oven. Serve cold.'

We would advise the following details for the 21st-century cook.

1. Preheat the oven to 140°C/gas mark 1.

2. Distribute the meat and seasoning evenly in the dish. If the consommé is very cold and therefore jellied, warm it in a saucepan. Pour the consommé over the meat and add a couple of tablespoons of sherry or brandy, if you like. Halfway through pouring, move the meat around a bit with a long sharp knife or spatula or skewer so that the consommé fills the crevices. Continue to pour in enough to cover the meat.

3. Put the dish in the oven, covered loosely with baking parchment and then a layer of foil. Bake long and slow for about 2 hours or until the meat is tender when pierced with a knife. Remove from the oven. Cool and then refrigerate. The consommé will set and become a jelly.

4. Serve cold or at room temperature straight from the dish, surrounded by Melba toast (see page 24). Sprinkle the terrine with some chopped fresh flat-leaf parsley in memory of Hilda.

NOTE: A fast version of this can be made utilising any leftover cooked game. Take the meat off the joint/bird. Cut or pull into nice pieces approx. 5cm in size. As before, put the meat in a terrine dish. Warm the consommé and add the seasoning and sherry. Pour this over the meat and put in the fridge to set. You can freeze this and defrost in the fridge. Ensure that you wrap it well.

VEAL AND HAM PIE

This is inspired by Jane Grigson's recipe from her 1974 bestseller *English Food*. The most appealing thing about it, for our purposes, is that the hot water crust pastry is a cinch to make, even for those with a phobia of rolling pins. The jelly is optional but equally straightforward. Don't be put off by the word 'gelatine', which has everyone thinking of slaughtered horses and fiddling about in the kitchen with sticky substances: leaf gelatine is easily found in supermarkets and simply adds a few minutes work to the overall preparation. Finally, on an ethical note, rose veal is humanely reared these days and buying it will support our farmers.

EQUIPMENT

18cm cake tin with removable
    base

♦ INGREDIENTS ♦

Serves 6

For the pastry
175ml lard
500g plain flour
½ teaspoon salt
1 egg, beaten

For the filling
750g pie veal, chopped into
    1cm pieces
375g unsmoked bacon or
    gammon (uncooked) in a
    piece, chopped into 1cm pieces
2 teaspoons lemon zest
1 tablespoon chopped fresh
    flat-leaf parsley
1 tablespoon chopped thyme
plenty of salt and freshly
    ground black pepper

For the jelly (optional)
500ml good-quality stock –
    chicken or veal or ham
4 leaves gelatine

Ideally, make the pie the day before you need it, as the flavour improves overnight.

(1) To make the pastry: put 200ml water with the lard in a saucepan and bring to the boil. Meanwhile sift the flour and salt into a large bowl and make a well in the centre. Tip the boiling water/lard mixture into the well and bring together using a wooden spoon or an electric whisk. When it is smooth, cover with a cloth and leave to cool down enough for you to handle it. Do not allow to get cold.

(2) Cut off a quarter of the dough (this will be the lid) and roll it out to about 20cm diameter – the size of the cake tin, plus a couple of centimetres. Press the remaining dough into the base of the cake tin and up the sides.

(3) Preheat oven to 200°C/gas mark 6.

(4) Put all the filling ingredients into a large bowl and stir well to combine. Pile into the pastry case and top with the circle of pastry you rolled out. Trim any excess pastry and use it to make leaves, etc. to decorate the case. Seal all the seams with beaten egg and press together. Make a hole in the middle for steam to escape. Glaze the surface with more egg.

(5) Bake in the oven for 30 minutes, then reduce the temperature to 160°C/gas mark 3 and bake for 1 hour. Remove the pie from the oven and let it cool in the tin for 30 minutes. Unmould and brush the sides with any remaining egg and return to the oven to glaze for 10 minutes.

(6) To make the optional jelly filling: heat the stock in a saucepan – do not let it boil. Meanwhile, soak the gelatine leaves in a little cold water for a couple of minutes. Squeeze them out and drop into the hot stock to melt. Stir thoroughly to ensure that the gelatine is evenly distributed and pour into the – now beautifully glazed – pie through the steam vent. This is easiest using a funnel but you can improvise with foil or baking parchment. The meat will have shrunk and the jelly fills in the gaps nicely – it will take a couple of hours to cool and set.

TOP-NOTCH EGGS

Why they were ever called Scotch Eggs is anyone's guess, as the origins of this tasty British picnic snack stretch back to the Indian subcontinent, where a dish called *nargisi kofta* was made by encasing a hard-boiled egg in spiced meat. Fortnum & Mason claim to have invented the Scotch Egg as we know it in 1738, and who are we to doubt such a reputable victualler? Our version is made with quails' eggs, so the finished result is smaller, more elegant and easily popped into the mouth during a picnic or at the high-tea table.

EQUIPMENT

Wok or heavy-bottomed
    saucepan

◆ INGREDIENTS ◆

Makes 12, golf-ball size

12 quails' eggs, soft-boiled and
    peeled (see page 65)
350g your favourite sausages,
    slipped out of their skins
pinch of mace
scraping of nutmeg
1 teaspoon your favourite mustard
¼ teaspoon anchovy paste
salt and freshly ground black
    pepper

For the coating
4 tablespoons milk
3 tablespoons flour
2 eggs, lightly beaten
100g breadcrumbs – fresh or
    use Panko crumbs

oil, for deep frying

(1) When preparing the eggs, drain and run under very cold water for a good 5 minutes. This will make them easier to peel. Ensure you remove all the shell. Dry the eggs on kitchen paper.

(2) Put the sausage meat in a bowl and add the spices, mustard and anchovy paste. Season and mix well until combined.

(3) Divide the mixture into 12. If you are a fanatic you can weigh them. Squish each one into a flat patty and wrap around each quail's egg to make a nice even ball.

(4) For the coating, pour the milk, flour, beaten eggs and breadcrumbs into 4 separate small bowls. To coat each parcel you need to dip and shake off the excess between each dip: first milk, then flour, then egg, then breadcrumbs. This forms a good seal coating and gives a good crunch.

(5) Heat the oil to 180°C in a wok or large, heavy-bottomed saucepan (you can judge the heat by frying a cube of bread: the oil is at the right temperature when the bread turns golden within a couple of seconds). Deep-fry the top-notch eggs in small batches so as not to reduce the temperature too much, which would make them soak up the oil and go soggy. They are done when they are a deep golden colour all over. Remove with a slotted spoon and drain on kitchen paper. Keep in the fridge until needed – for up to 3 days.

 SAFETY NOTE: When deep-frying, have ready a baking tray that fits over the diameter of the pan in which you are frying. In the event of a fire, chuck it on the pan – it will smother the flames.

STILTON STRAWS

If making these in advance, bake them just before your guests arrive: they are heavenly served hot, crisp and molten from the oven. As well as for high tea, Stilton Straws make an ideal snack, with a nice hot chocolate, for elevenses. Take some into the office and watch your colleagues crowd around your desk, eschewing their muesli bars and KitKats for something much more wholesome, refined and steeped in flavour. Stilton Straws freeze very well, so make an extra batch and put them in the freezer at the raw stage. To bake them from frozen, simply allow an extra 5 minutes or so baking time. These are 'blow your socks off' strong – the faint-hearted may choose to reduce the mustard.

EQUIPMENT

Grater or food-processor
   (optional)

◆ INGREDIENTS ◆

Serves 4

1 sheet ready-rolled puff
   pastry
6 tablespoons mustard (any
   sort, including English
   mustard) – if using powdered,
   make up with water
   or port
10 anchovy fillets or 5
   teaspoons anchovy paste,
   whichever you have to hand
180g Stilton
lots of freshly ground black
   pepper

The fun part (optional)
You can add more than a smattering
of anything else you like: dried or fresh
herbs, your favourite spices (caraway
seeds work well), a sprinkle of
Worcestershire sauce, redcurrant sauce
or a favourite chutney, damson cheese or
quince marmalade.

(1)   Preheat oven to 200°C/gas mark 6.

(2)   Lay out the sheet of puff pastry on a chopping board. Paint on mustard across the entire top two thirds by dolloping on large amounts and using a knife or the back of a spoon to spread it.

(3)   Tear up the anchovy fillets and dot around or spread on anchovy paste. Top with crumbled Stilton. If you have a grater or food-processor, you can finely chop up the rind and old hard bits left over from your Christmas truckle – or add in any old cheese lurking in your fridge. Sprinkle with plenty of black pepper.

(4)   Now fold the bottom empty third up over the middle third – as if folding a letter. Next fold the last third over the remainder to make a nice parcel with two good layers of filling. If you have a rolling pin (or empty claret bottle) to hand, you could give it a gentle rolling at this point, just to squish it all nicely together. Otherwise, just press gently with your hands.

(5)   If you have time, chill it, still on the board, for a few minutes in the fridge to firm up while you clear the decks.

(6)   Using a large sharp knife, cut into straws, approx. 2cm each. Lay them, marbled centres uppermost, on a baking tray. No need to line the sheet – puff pastry is so fatty it won't stick. However, if you use baking parchment (not greaseproof, not foil), you'll have less washing up. Bake for 12–15 minutes. The straws will be soft when they first come out of the oven but will harden as they cool. It is easier to wait a moment before taking them off the baking tray.

(7)   Transfer them to a nice dish or basket for serving. Your guests will hoover them up, so make plenty.

PICKLED ONIONS

Before you start chucking these into your Dry Martinis to make a Gibson, these are the larger variety of pickled onion (Gibsons take pickled silverskin onions). The whole point of these, as any fish and chip vendor will tell you, is to offer a tart, crunchy balance for heavier, saltier flavours. Yes, you can buy them ready-made, and the ones you can buy are perfectly good, but the process of making them yourself is easy, fun and satisfying. We suggest you start with this fairly small quantity, then graduate to larger batches, as you can multiply up the amounts as many times as you like.

◆ INGREDIENTS ◆

Makes 1 500ml jar

250g small pickling onions
    or shallots
½ teaspoon mustard seed
½ teaspoon black
    peppercorns
1 bay leaf
250ml malt vinegar – or
    cider/wine vinegar if you
    prefer less strong flavour

① Sterilise your jar and its lid by putting them through a hot dishwasher cycle. Bring them out when dry, and secure the lid to keep the jar sterile. Use whenever you are ready. Otherwise, give the jar and lid a good scrub inside and out with a brush and hot soapy water. Rinse jolly well. Now put in the oven at 120°C/gas mark ½ for 10 minutes to dry. Put the lid on and let the jar cool before using.

② If the onions prove tricky to peel, put them into a bowl or saucepan and pour boiling water over them. Let sit for 20 seconds. Drain and plunge into ice water. Now skin them – the skins should slip off easily.

③ Pile the onions into your jar, adding the mustard seeds, black peppercorns and bay leaf as you go along so they are nicely distributed. Pour over the cold vinegar – right to the top.

④ Seal and put into a dark, cool place to cure for a minimum of 4 weeks. They will be much better if left for 8 weeks or longer.

This is a lovely little snack to offer at Christmas. If you like spicy fragrant flavours, you could add some cloves to the pickling mix. If you like your pickles soft rather than crisp, heat the vinegar before adding to the jar. If you like them sweet, add 45g sugar with the spices.

CHAP'S CHUTNEY

In Henry Moses' 1850 tome *Sketches of India*, we can gauge the wide popularity of mango chutney during the height of the British Raj: 'The number of mangoes that a practised person may eat with impunity is really astonishing. A little pale brandy is taken afterwards by way of security and a bath to get rid of the jaundiced complexion is sometimes absolutely necessary.' Since then, the British have calmed down their enthusiasm for mango chutney and dozens of other chutneys have emerged. Ours is a classic old-world recipe that uses the sorts of dried fruits once newly arriving in England along the Silk Route, as well as green tomatoes, which limp British summers can ensure are often plentiful.

◆INGREDIENTS◆

Makes 1 750ml jar

110g dates, roughly chopped
110g raisins
140g apple, grated or finely chopped
140g green tomatoes, chopped
110g brown sugar
150ml malt vinegar – or you can use wine or cider for a less tangy chutney

① Sterilise your jar and its lid by putting them through a hot dishwasher cycle. Bring them out when dry and secure the lid to keep the jar sterile. Use whenever you are ready. Otherwise, give the jar and lid a good scrub inside and out with a brush and hot soapy water. Rinse jolly well. Now put in the oven at 120°C/gas mark ½ for 10 minutes to dry. Put the lid on and let the jar cool before using.

② Stir all the ingredients except vinegar together in a bowl to combine. Pack into the jar, top up with vinegar and seal. Store in a dark place. Turn and shake the contents from time to time. Keep for 3 months before opening.

UNBAKED CAKE
FOR RUM COVES

Every chap should have this cake in his repertoire. You can assemble it in a few minutes without so much as turning on the oven and no one will know you haven't been slaving away all day over it. When a maiden aunt suddenly announces her imminent arrival the following Sunday with a string of nephews, one of whom is celebrating their birthday, this is a much better option than dashing out for a stale Mr Kipling from the corner shop. This is an assembly job that requires no oven or special equipment.

EQUIPMENT

Grater or food-processor
    (optional)

◆ INGREDIENTS ◆

*Serves 8–12, depending on greed/
generosity of slices*

600ml double cream – icy cold so
    it whips quickly and well
410g tin condensed milk
1 teaspoon vanilla extract, if
    you have it
200ml strong coffee
50ml rum (or an extra 50ml
    coffee for a non-alcoholic
    version)
32 butter biscuits

*To decorate (optional)
Birthday candles and other suitable
decorations, such as edible rose petals,
gold leaf, grated chocolate or hundreds
and thousands.*

① Line a cake, loaf or biscuit tin, even a straight-sided saucepan – it is only a cake shape you are after – with clingfilm. The clingfilm means you can get the cake out more easily.

② Whisk together the cream, condensed milk and vanilla until thick soft peaks are formed. Don't overwhisk. The peaks should hold their shape but fall after a second. Soft and fluffy is better than hard.

③ Pour a thick layer – 3cm or so – into the base of the lined mould and spread evenly.

④ Mix the coffee and rum in a bowl. Dip each biscuit briefly in the liquid and arrange a layer of biscuits on the cream mixture base. Now alternate between biscuit and cream layers until all used up. Wrap in clingfilm and leave for a minimum of 4 hours, or preferably overnight.

⑤ To serve, remove the clingfilm covering the top. Invert onto a nice plate or cake stand, peel off the clingfilm and bask in the appreciative gasps. If it is someone's birthday, stud it with candles and sprinkle with rose petals, gold leaf, grated chocolate or hundreds and thousands, depending on age of recipient.

COCKTAILS

It has become fashionable in recent years to make cocktails at home. This is as ridiculous as trying to cut your own hair or give your own car an MOT test. But there is another reason, apart from the perfectly good one of leaving cocktails for experts to make for you in stylish bars, and that is because cocktails are the wrong drinks to serve before a meal. Constance Spry and Rosemary Hume, writing in *Hostess* in 1961, went so far as to suggest that people doing so would be regarded as 'savages'. Today, it may take a bit more than offering someone a Manhattan to be branded a savage, but a much more suitable aperitif would be a glass of Madeira, dry sherry or Amontillado. This will cleanse the palate sufficiently and relax your guests before sitting down to eat, rather than 'sharpening the appetite', which, given the strength of some spirits today, really means 'make you so drunk that you'll eat anything'.

— CHAPTER 5 —

DINNER

The very fact that every region in Britain seems to have its own particular word for the evening meal is testament to its cultural significance. Our way of avoiding all the snobbery associated with it was to source all our recipes exclusively from either country houses or gentlemen's clubs, where it is always called 'dinner'. And if you think that this means eight courses and eight different forks for each guest, you'd be right – although, due to reasons of space, we have limited ourselves here to two courses, followed by pudding (see Chapter 8).

PARTAN BREE

This elegant and delicious soup originates from northeastern Scotland, its name a combination of the Gaelic for crab (*partan*) and the northeastern Scots or Doric dialect for soup (*bree*). Partan Bree is light, yet full flavoured, smoky, yet fresh. Traditionally it contains no alcohol, although a glug of whisky brings out all the flavours so beautifully it is worth breaking the rules – few Scots will mind the addition of a spot of the local tipple.

EQUIPMENT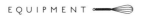

Stick blender

♦ INGREDIENTS ♦

Serves 8

30g butter
175g white rice
600ml full-fat milk
600ml fish stock (or vegetable
    stock)
50ml whisky
½ teaspoon anchovy purée
¼ teaspoon mace
pinch of cayenne
1 large cooked crab, white and
    brown meat, or either if
    preferred
450ml single cream
handful of fresh flat-leaf
    parsley, chopped
toast, to serve

(1) Melt the butter in a saucepan, add the rice and stir it around until coated and slightly toasted.

(2) Add the milk, stock, whisky, anchovy purée, mace and cayenne. Bring to the boil, then turn down the heat and simmer for 20 minutes, until the rice is cooked soft.

(3) Liquidise in the pan with a stick blender until smooth. Stir in the crabmeat and cream. Warm through and taste for seasoning.

(4) Serve hot with chopped fresh flat-leaf parsley and toast.

BROWN WINDSOR SOUP

Though familiar to anyone who has ever watched *Fawlty Towers*, or even stayed in a similar establishment where Brown Windsor Soup is always on the menu, there is little evidence that it was ever more than just a joke. White Windsor Soup appears in Escoffier's 1903 edition, but there is no official record of the Brown variety appearing anywhere until the 1950s. Even British Rail menus bear no trace of this supposedly classic English Victorian soup, so perhaps it really was invented by the *Goon Show*? Nevertheless, Brown Windsor is still worth recreating, as it is a delicious, beefy, hearty, dark soup that would revive even a bedridden Basil Fawlty himself.

EQUIPMENT

Stick blender

◆ INGREDIENTS ◆

Serves 8

50g butter
300g stewing steak, cut into
    3cm pieces and dried on
    kitchen paper so they will
    brown
1 onion, chopped
2 sticks celery, chopped
1 small carrot, chopped
2 tablespoons flour
1 teaspoon tomato purée
1 teaspoon thyme leaves
2 fresh bay leaves
3 litres beef stock
50ml sherry
salt and freshly ground black
    pepper

(1) Melt the butter in a large saucepan and add the meat to brown. Then tip in all the vegetables and stir to coat and cook for a couple of minutes.

(2) Sprinkle in the flour and stir well. Add the purée, herbs and beef stock. Stir well to combine.

(3) Bring to the boil and simmer uncovered for 2 hours – longer if necessary; the liquid should reduce by half. Using a stick blender, blend a little to thicken, but not too much.

(4) Pour in the sherry and taste for seasoning before serving.

LONDON PARTICULAR

A fast, easy soup that you can make from stuff in your cupboards and freezer, named after the infamous fog of London during the Victorian period that was also referred to as a 'pea souper'. Lettuce, although not usually found at the back of a cupboard (if it is, now you know what that smell was) is a welcome addition to this soup, if not essential – although lettuce and peas are a classic British combination, as they grow well together in the vegetable garden.

◆ INGREDIENTS ◆

Serves 6

600ml stock or water plus a
    stock cube – chicken is best
1 medium potato, roughly
    chopped into approx.
    2cm pieces
2 shallots
300ml milk or single or double
    cream (or a mixture, if you
    prefer)
1 head of lettuce (optional),
    roughly chopped
a handful of dill, tarragon,
    lovage or flat-leaf parsley, or
    a sprig of each
300g frozen peas
6 eggs (optional)

(1) Put all the ingredients except the peas and eggs in a saucepan – peas go in at the end to stay bright green. Bring to the boil, then turn down the heat and simmer for 10 minutes. Add the peas and stir until thawed. Purée with a stick blender until smooth and velvety.

(2) If you or your guests are particularly hungry, crack a fresh egg for each person into the soup and poach until cooked. Serve in soup plates – without bread, unless you want to spoil the main course.

DUCK TERRINE

Terrines are notoriously fiddly, which is the last thing you need when the guests are queuing up at the kitchen door for their aperitifs. We wanted to create a terrine with the minimum of ingredients and fuss: no breadcrumbs, no frying of meat or shallots, no wrapping with bacon. Simply a series of layers, meaty and spiced, leaving you ample time to ensure that your guests are well lubricated and also to attend to the main course. You don't even need a food-processor for this, although it will help; all you really need is a good sharp chopping knife. The result is a very dense and rich meaty terrine, of which a little goes a long way. Serve with a good chutney or jelly, And toast, preferably Melba – see page 24. The rule with terrines is always to make them 24 hours before you need them, although this one is perfectly fine made in the morning in time for a teatime picnic or gathering.

EQUIPMENT

Either a terrine dish, crock, baking
    dish or loaf or cake tin – it
    should have 1-litre capacity and
    be 6cm or more in height, to
    look suitably impressive – or
    individual dariole moulds or
    muffin tins

♦ INGREDIENTS ♦

Serves 8

dab of butter, for greasing
5 pickled walnuts (optional),
    sliced
2 duck breasts
250g pork shoulder
100g chicken livers, trimmed
good pinch of mace
good pinch of celery salt
good pinch of sea salt
good pinch of cinnamon
½ teaspoon ground black
    peppercorns
dash of brandy (optional)
melted butter, pink
    peppercorns or sliced
    pickled walnuts and bay leaf,
    to serve (optional)
Melba toast, to serve

1) Preheat oven to 160°C/gas mark 3. Butter the dish or moulds and line the base with sliced pickled walnuts, if using.

2) Put the duck, pork, chicken livers, spices, seasoning and brandy (if using) in a food-processor and chop finely.

3) Fill the dish with the meat mixture. Scrunch up a sheet of baking parchment, unfurl and spread out over the top of the dish. Seal with a layer of foil. Place in a roasting tin and then put it in the oven. Pull the oven shelf halfway out (hold it carefully) and half-fill the roasting tin with water. Carefully push the shelf back in, close oven and bake the terrine for 1¼ hours.

4) Remove from the oven. This is the important bit: you need to weight it while it cools. A couple of unopened cans will do the trick, or old-fashioned kitchen weights placed on top of the foil. When cool, transfer it to the fridge.

5) Remove from the fridge a couple of hours before you wish to serve. The flavours must be allowed to develop and the texture will be better if the terrine is not fridge cold.

6) To serve, you can turn it out onto a pretty serving plate or take it to the table in its cooking dish. It looks pretty if you pour a little melted butter – leaving the milk deposits in the saucepan – over the surface and sprinkle over a few pink peppercorns or sliced pickled walnuts and maybe a bay leaf to become submerged and encased within the butter.

This dish keeps for a week in the fridge, well wrapped, and the flavour improves. It also freezes very well for a month.

CHICKEN LIVER PÂTÉ
WITH GIN AND JUNIPER

There is something reassuringly old fashioned about pâté. You know it's old fashioned when hardly anybody orders it from the menu in a restaurant, citing that it's 'too filling' or 'too meaty'. Which is precisely why we offer it here. Ours is a particularly meaty version made from chicken livers, with the added frisson (and another reason for non-chaps to eschew it) of gin, giving the pâté an invigorating zing that other pâtés do not have.

EQUIPMENT

Blender or food-processor

◆ INGREDIENTS ◆

Serves 8

300g chicken livers –
    organic, for obvious reasons
50g butter
2 shallots, roughly chopped
2 tablespoons gin
2 juniper berries, crushed,
    plus a few extra for
    decoration if you like
1 bay leaf, crushed or very
    finely chopped, and a whole
    one for decoration, if you
    like
pinch of mace
1 tablespoon honey
100ml cream – any sort
plenty of salt and freshly
    ground black pepper

(1) Wash and dry the chicken livers, halve lengthways and snip out the cores.

(2) Melt the butter in a frying pan, add the shallots and soften for a few minutes. Add the chicken livers and brown nicely on all sides – about 4 minutes.

(3) Pour in the gin and scrape up all the bits and juices in the pan. Add the juniper, bay leaf, seasoning, mace, honey and cream. Let bubble for a minute while stirring.

(4) Tip the whole lot into a blender or food-processor. Whizz up as smooth as you like. Pour into a dish and smooth the top. If you are turning it out, line the dish with clingfilm to make it easier. Decorate the top with a few juniper berries and bay leaf. Cover and put in the fridge to chill – it will keep for 3 days.

SCALLOP SUNSET

A recipe inspired by Jane Grigson (mother of Sophie Grigson), a contemporary of Elizabeth David. Jane provided middle England with their staple diet for decades, particularly during the 1970s, when she offered a more sensible contrast to the chaotic – although equally appealing to chaps – methods of Keith Floyd. The rich colours of this dish make it easy on the eye when served, which can be with slices or purée of cooked beetroot – which Grigson described as 'far too bossy a vegetable, unless you have a mediaeval passion for brightly-coloured food'.

EQUIPMENT

Blender or food processor

♦ INGREDIENTS ♦

Serves 4

50ml white wine
300ml fish stock
zest and juice of ½ orange
16 scallops
45g samphire or tiny, pencil-
    thin asparagus
a little freshly ground black
    pepper (no salt – the
    samphire will provide this)

① Put the wine, stock and orange zest and juice in a frying pan or wide saucepan over a medium heat and let bubble for 5 minutes.

② Throw in the scallops and samphire (or asparagus, if using) and poach for 4–6 minutes. Take them out and keep warm on a dish.

③ Increase the heat and boil rapidly to reduce the liquor by a third. Taste and adjust seasoning as necessary.

④ Pour the sauce over the dish and serve.

WINE ETIQUETTE

If you are invited to a dinner party, there is an assumption that one should bring a bottle of wine and this can lead to hours of agonising in one's local victualler over the balance between price and vintage. The simple solution is not to bring any wine at all: it is considered vulgar and an insult to your host's wine cellar. Instead, bring flowers. Conversely, if a guest brings a bottle of wine to your dinner party, deftly take it into the kitchen, making no remark at all except 'Thank you'. Decant it into your crystal decanter and serve, along with several other wines in decanters. Wine one-upmanship and discussions as to who brought what are not an important element of any social gathering.

CHARIOTS OF SAMPHIRE

Samphire, as we mentioned in our Lunch menu, is a neglected British vegetable that speaks of the sea in a thoroughly British way: windswept shores, craggy cliffs, blustery walks and meals in seaside cottages while storms rage outside. Your guests will immediately be transported there, whether on holiday or not, if you serve them this colourful dish. If the weather is calm outside, then give everyone a large seashell to clamp to one ear while they eat. They'll get the idea.

EQUIPMENT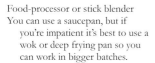

Food-processor or stick blender
You can use a saucepan, but if
you're impatient it's best to use a
wok or deep frying pan so you
can work in bigger batches.

♦ INGREDIENTS ♦

Serves 4–6

90g samphire, rinsed and
dried well
500ml groundnut or rapeseed
oil, for frying

For the batter:
100ml ice-cold water
120ml ice-cold vodka
1 large egg yolk
110g plain flour

**For the St Clements mayo
(can be made up to 2 days
in advance)**
1 egg
zest and juice of ½ lemon
zest and juice of ½ orange
1 teaspoon mustard
200ml groundnut oil or
good rapeseed oil
pinch of salt and freshly
ground black pepper

Before you begin, have everything ready in the kitchen and ensure the samphire is properly dry.

(1) Begin by making the mayonnaise. If you have a food-processor, use it. Put all the ingredients except the oil in the bowl and whizz together. Now start adding the oil in a steady stream as you whizz. If you only have a stick blender, proceed as above. You just need a steady hand to drizzle the oil down the side of the jug. Taste and adjust the seasoning. Chill until needed. This will last up to 2 days in the fridge.

(2) Next make the batter. The secret to good, light, crisp batter is temperature – you want it icy cold. Put the mixing bowl containing the ice-cold water and vodka into the freezer for 20 minutes to ensure it is freezing. A butter knife is ideal for stirring. Put that in the freezer too.

(3) Meanwhile, fill your pan of choice with oil to a depth of about 2cm and heat the oil to 190°C. To test the temperature, throw in a few cubes of bread – they should turn golden brown within 50–60 seconds.

(4) Take the bowl of water and vodka out of the freezer. Add the egg yolk and stir well to mix. Tip in the flour and stir with the knife just barely to combine. Don't worry about lumps. The less stirring, the crisper your batter will be. If in doubt, stir less and test one to see.

(5) Working quickly and in batches, ideally using tongs (easier than fingers), dip the samphire in the batter and then drop into the hot oil. Allow to fry for a minute or so until golden. Remove from the oil, briefly blot on kitchen paper and then straight onto a warm serving dish. Keep going until you've fried all the samphire. Serve immediately.

STALKER'S PIE

Asuperb recipe for using up leftovers from other recipes in this book. The name may imply stalking across the moors in damp tweeds, but really you will be stalking about the kitchen in search of leftover gravy, root vegetables, the green parts of spring onions, the odd mushroom and finely chopped parsley stalks. Don't be put off by the title – it's only a pie in the sense that Shepherd's Pie is – but a far more satisfying, impressive and fortifying dish and not one you can buy as a frozen ready meal.

EQUIPMENT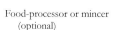

Food-processor or mincer
(optional)

◆ INGREDIENTS ◆

Serves 4

For the filling
50g butter
1 large onion, finely chopped
2 celery sticks, finely chopped
2 large carrots, cut into approx.
    2.5cm chunks
1 bay leaf
2 sprigs of thyme
300g pork mince
2 glasses cider or wine
dash of sherry/port/brandy
300g leftover cooked venison,
    finely chopped or minced
500ml beef or chicken stock or
    500ml water plus 2 stock
    cubes – 1 beef, 1 vegetable
2 tablespoons redcurrant
    jelly/sauce
½ jar pickled walnuts, drained
    and quartered

For the topping:
800g very small potatoes,
    preferably with red skins
300ml single cream
100g butter
5 tablespoons grainy mustard
good scraping of nutmeg
salt and freshly ground black
    pepper

(1) For the filling: melt the butter in a large saucepan and then add onion, celery, carrots, bay leaf and thyme. Stir well and let it all sweat for 5 minutes.

(2) Put the pork mince into a separate frying pan over a high heat and fry off until browned and crispy.

(3) Keeping the heat high, pour over the cider or wine and the dash of sherry, port or brandy to deglaze the pan, scraping up all the lovely sticky bits from the base of the pan. Turn off the heat and tip the whole lot into the saucepan with the vegetables. Add the venison, stock, redcurrant jelly or sauce and pickled walnuts. Stir well and let it simmer gently for 45 minutes, lid half-on to stop all the liquid evaporating. Give it a stir from time to time.

(4) For the topping: put the potatoes, whole, into another large saucepan and cover with cold water. Add a pinch of salt, cover with the lid and bring to the boil. Turn down and simmer for approx. 30 minutes, until tender when pierced with a sharp knife. Drain, return to the pan and shake over a very low heat to dry, then, using the back of a wooden spoon, crush each potato until it pops.

(5) Pour in the cream, butter, grainy mustard, nutmeg and salt and pepper. Fold in gently until just incorporated but leaving the potatoes rustically rough-textured – you are not aiming for mash.

(6) Check the meat mixture for seasoning and add extra if needed. Turn the meat mixture into a baking dish and top with the crushed potato mixture. Brown under a hot grill or in a hot oven for approx. 20 minutes. The dish will keep warm in the oven for 45 minutes or so at 120°C/gas mark ½. Serve on its own or with salad or vegetables.

LAMB CUTLETS
WITH REFORM CLUB SAUCE

The Reform Club on Pall Mall in London is the quintessential gentlemen's club. It is the one used in films whenever a location is required to show crusty old duffers smoking cigars and harrumphing over their broadsheet newspapers. The dining room is legendary and the experience of dining there is a little like going back to schooldays – if you are an old Etonian. The Reform Club Lamb Cutlets have been on their menu since being created by Alexis Soyer in the 1830s, allegedly to satisfy a member who demanded dinner at some ungodly hour, and Soyer had to make do with limited ingredients.

◆ INGREDIENTS ◆

Serves 2

6 well-trimmed lamb cutlets –
    ask your butcher to prepare
    them for you
1 egg, beaten
75g fresh breadcrumbs
50g butter
1 tablespoon sunflower or
    vegetable oil
plenty of salt and freshly
    ground black pepper

For the Reform Club sauce
2 tablespoons wine vinegar
2 tablespoons sugar – any
    sort, but brown is best
1 tablespoon black
    peppercorns, crushed
1 shallot, chopped
300ml stock – beef, lamb,
    chicken or game
1 tablespoon redcurrant jelly
50g ham, cut into matchsticks
2 tablespoons finely chopped
    cooked beetroot – can be
    pickled
2 small gherkins, finely
    chopped
1 hard-boiled egg white, finely
    chopped

(1) Ensure the lamb is well trimmed and the bones are nicely scraped and clean. Bring the cutlets out of the fridge, season well with salt and pepper and allow to come to room temperature 1 hour before cooking.

(2) Meanwhile, make the sauce. Put the vinegar, sugar, peppercorns and shallot in a medium saucepan. Bring to the boil and simmer for 20 minutes. Pour in the stock, bring to the boil and simmer for 5 minutes.

(3) Now back to the cutlets. Pour the beaten egg and the breadcrumbs into two separate shallow bowls. Dip the cutlets first in the egg, then the breadcrumbs and ensure they are nicely coated. Heat the butter and oil in a frying pan and fry the cutlets for about 4 minutes on each side. Keep warm on a serving plate to let the meat rest while you finish the sauce.

(4) To finish the sauce, strain it into a clean saucepan, add the remaining ingredients and bring to the boil. Serve immediately with the cutlets, piping hot.

ROAST PHEASANT
AND GAME CHIPS

Dorothy Hartley, in her seminal 1954 tome, *Food in England*, advises us to catch a pheasant by hiding some raisins in a paper bag and lurking among the peas in your garden. 'When he sticks his head in he cannot see where to go, so he stands still till you fetch him.' Easier said than done, in today's more lily-livered world, so you may have to go and buy a pheasant that a farmer has already 'fetched' for you. You must ensure the pheasant you buy is well hung, otherwise you may as well buy a chicken. The main exercise with pheasant is to stop it from drying out (see Note below); if it could be cooked underwater, we would tell you how.

EQUIPMENT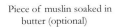

Piece of muslin soaked in
    butter (optional)

♦ INGREDIENTS ♦

Serves 2

1 pheasant, rinsed
100–150g soft butter
a few sprigs of thyme
1 small onion or shallot,
    halved
a few random vegetables on
    which to sit the bird to roast
    it – celery and carrots are good
50ml wine or water
salt and freshly ground black
    pepper

For the brining solution
1 litre water
450g sea salt
1 shallot, halved
1 teaspoon whole peppercorns
4 sprigs of fresh flat-leaf
    parsley
2 sprigs of thyme

For the game chips
200g waxy potatoes (look for
    'salad potatoes')
vegetable or sunflower oil
or
good-quality potato
    crisps

(1) Pheasant can be dry, so here we do everything we can to make it succulent. Mix the brining solution and immerse the bird – a large freezer bag is good for this – for 1 hour minimum, 6 hours maximum, in the fridge or a suitably cold place. Take out the bird, rinse and dry it, and let it come up to room temperature.

(2) Preheat oven to 190°C/gas mark 5.

(3) Slather the entire bird in soft butter and sprinkle over salt and pepper. Put more butter inside the cavity, season with salt and pepper and add the thyme and an onion or shallot, which will add more moisture, as well as flavour, from the inside.

(4) Put the vegetables in a roasting tin and sit the pheasant on top. Pour around the wine, avoiding the pheasant. Transfer to the oven and roast for 40 minutes. Baste regularly. Halfway through cooking, cover loosely with foil. Rest the bird for 15 minutes before serving. Keep it covered well so it stays super-hot.

(5) To make game chips: finely slice your waxy potatoes using the side of a cheese grater, or a mandolin if you have one. Rinse and thoroughly pat dry. Put in a bowl and pour over some vegetable or sunflower oil, salt and pepper and turn to coat. Spread them out on a baking tray or roasting tin. Roast in a hot oven (220°C/gas mark 7) for 40 minutes until crisp.

(6) You can cheat with game chips, which after all are really just hot crisps. Just use very good-quality crisps, such as Kettle Chips or Tyrells. Spread them out on a baking tray and bake for approx. 5 minutes at 180°C/gas mark 4 while the pheasant is resting.

Note: If you are very worried about your bird being dry, there are a few more things you can do during step 3 to preserve moisture. You can cover it with muslin soaked in butter. When basted, it keeps the juice on the bird rather than running off. You can wrap it in caul, a net-like fat, which will slowly baste the bird. You can put butter under the skin of the bird, over the breast. You can cover the breast with bacon, although the flavour will penetrate the bird – using unsmoked bacon is important, unless you want your bird to taste like a packet of smoky bacon crisps.

DUKE OF CUMBERLAND'S GAMMON

Gammon has been on a long journey from the time of Cato the Elder, who wrote heartily about the salting of hams in 160 BC, to the days when it languished on shelves in vacuum-packed parcels back in the 1970s, waiting to be topped with a canned pineapple ring. We're going to take it back closer to Cato the Elder's time. The best joint of gammon is a leg with the bone in it. Ask the butcher to show you a few and choose the nicest looking, then get him to trim it for you. This dish is ideal for feeding lots of people, and what's left can be served cold as ham. Leftover meat will keep for a week in the fridge. After that, take it off the bone in slices or chunks, use some for Eggs Cumberbatch (see page 15) and freeze the rest.

EQUIPMENT

A saucepan large enough to
   comfortably accommodate the
   gammon

♦ INGREDIENTS ♦

*Serves 20 people or more – allows for
plenty of leftovers in the larder*

approx. 4kg gammon joint
1 teaspoon whole cloves
1 teaspoon whole black
   peppercorns
2 bay leaves
1 onion, skin on and halved
2 sprigs of thyme or rosemary
   or flat-leaf parsley
sliver of lemon zest

For the glaze
5 tablespoons brown sugar
5 tablespoons mustard
4 tablespoons whole cloves

For the Cumberland sauce
340g jar redcurrant jelly
50ml port
zest and juice of 1 orange
zest and juice of 1 lemon

① Put the gammon in the saucepan and cover with cold water. Add the flavouring ingredients. Bring slowly to the boil and simmer for 20 minutes per 450g. Allow the gammon to cool a little in the liquid before you lift it out.

② Preheat oven to 200°C/gas mark 6. Lift the gammon out of the saucepan, pat dry, and place in a roasting tin. Using a small sharp knife, remove the leathery skin, but leave as much thick fat on the joint as you can.

③ A steady hand here: rub all over with the sugar and mustard – this will create a lovely flavoursome glaze. Score the fat into diamond patterns and stud the diamonds with cloves.

④ Put into the oven and roast for 30 minutes until the glaze is burnished, basting once or twice to ensure a lovely glaze. Allow the meat to rest for 20 minutes before serving.

⑤ To make the Cumberland sauce: put all the ingredients in a saucepan and heat gently until melted and bubbling. Serve hot or cold. It keeps very well, so put the leftovers into a clean jar, label, and use it for other things too. You can make the sauce weeks ahead.

KIDNEY IN A GREATCOAT

For offal connoisseurs, there is no finer part of the interior of an animal than the kidney. Here, the suet, usually cut off and turned into Christmas puddings, becomes the very oven itself, providing all its own juices integral to the kidney. You will have to put in a special request at your butcher to order you a kidney still in its own fat. If he can't help you, wander over to the nearest livestock farm, or go on the Internet and find a farmer who sells kidneys by post. If you are offered any kidneys that don't come from animals, quickly switch off your computer.

♦ INGREDIENTS ♦

Serves 1

1 lamb's kidney still in all its
   own fat (suet)
salt and freshly ground
   pepper

(1) This is actually at its best cooked on an open fire – or dare we suggest a barbecue (one of your unsophisticated relatives may have one in their garden). To cook in the kitchen: crank your oven up to 220°C/gas mark 7.

(2) Sit the kidney on a trivet in a roasting tin. Transfer to the oven and roast for 20 minutes.

(3) Serve immediately. It looks best served on a plain white linen napkin, or in a little dish on a plate. Your guest then breaks open the little fat jacket to reveal the moist, perfectly cooked kidney within. The kidney can be seasoned at will.

VENISON
WITH CREAM, MARSALA AND CHESTNUTS

This recipe is a celebration dish, designed to be shared with your warmest friends and closest family. If there are any maiden aunts on the way over, cook something else. Venison tends to veer towards the dry side, so this recipe uses brining – a perfect way to deal with meat that shies away from moistness in its natural state. Venison is also a generous meat: a 1.8kg haunch will easily serve 8 people. There is very little fat in venison (have you seen them bounding around?), so remind your guests that not only is this dish utterly mouth-watering, but it is also good for them.

EQUIPMENT

Large roasting tin
Meat thermometer (optional)
Trivet (optional)

♦ INGREDIENTS ♦

Serves 8–10

2kg venison haunch (bone in,
    if possible)
150g butter, softened
3 tablespoons groundnut or
    sunflower oil
good grind of black pepper
6 slices unsmoked streaky bacon
    or 200g caul (optional)

For the brine
2 litres water
90g sea salt
1 teaspoon each juniper
    berries, whole cloves,
    cinnamon powder (or grind
    some cinnamon sticks)
½ orange
1 wine glass Marsala

For the sauce
200g chestnuts, halved or
    roughly chopped; reserve a
    few whole ones for garnish
300ml single cream
150ml Marsala

(1) Make the brine by mixing all the ingredients together. Put in the venison and soak for a minimum 6 hours, maximum 12 hours.

(2) Preheat oven to 190°C/gas mark 5.

(3) Lift the venison out of the brine. Rinse and dry it well. Heat a large frying pan, add 50g of the butter and the groundnut or sunflower oil (which stops the butter burning). Quickly brown the meat all over in the hot pan.

(4) Rub the remainder of the soft butter all over the meat and grind on plenty of black pepper. Wrap in caul or cover with bacon if you are using it.

(5) Place in a roasting tin in which you have put some vegetables or a trivet to stop the meat frying on the bottom. Cover loosely with parchment and then foil. Roast for 15 minutes per kilo. A meat thermometer is useful for this dish: the temperature should read 60°C when the probe is inserted into the thickest part. Cook until the right temperature is reached.

(6) When cooked, remove from the oven and cover with foil, adding a few extra layers of tea-towel to keep it really warm. Let the meat rest for 15–20 minutes – this step is vital.

(7) To make the sauce: put the chestnuts, cream and Marsala in a saucepan and boil for 2 minutes. You can add the roasting juices from the meat to the sauce if you like, or serve them separately. There is virtually no fat in the juices, so no need to skim.

(8) To serve, transfer the venison haunch to a beautiful serving plate. Discard the vegetables and pour the juices into a serving jug – unless you added them to the Marsala sauce.

This dish is very good with Chap's Mashed Potato (see page 114) and Braised Baby Lettuce (see page 118). The braised lettuce stops the dish being overwhelmingly rich.

DEERSTALKER'S REWARD

Deer are currently being culled at the enormous rate of 50–60 per cent, in order to keep the deer population stable. Without natural predators such as brown bears and wolves, the deer just keep on reproducing at an alarming rate, so it is actually humane to cull them. This is of course good news for the chap's dinner table, as decent venison is becoming readily available and cheap. The sloe gin marinates the tough venison meat for up to 12 hours, making for a succulent, rich, boozy dish, perfect after an afternoon's stalking. You can use leftover roasted venison for this if you like – just skip the marinating process.

◆ INGREDIENTS ◆

Serves 6–8

1.5kg venison, any cut, cut
   into 5cm chunks
150ml sloe gin
10 blackberries, crushed
50g butter
50ml vegetable or rapeseed oil
300ml chicken stock
300ml beef or venison
   stock
100g blackberries, plus a
   few extra to serve
salt and freshly ground
   black pepper

(1) Put the venison in a bowl or large freezer bag. Season with a little salt and pepper and pour in the sloe gin and the 10 crushed blackberries. Marinate for 2 hours (at room temperature) or overnight (in the fridge).

(2) Preheat oven to 160°C/gas mark 3.

(3) Take the venison out of the marinade – reserve the marinade for later. Pat the venison dry. You will need the meat to be dry so it will brown nicely.

(4) Melt the butter and oil in an ovenproof casserole dish and brown the venison chunks in batches, setting them aside as they are done.

(5) Deglaze the pan with the marinade juices and let them bubble while you scrape any brown bits off the bottom of the dish.

(6) Put the venison into the dish and pour over both types of stock. Add the blackberries. Stir well and put in the oven to bake for 1½ hours, or until the meat is tender.

(7) Check liquid for seasoning. Scatter some fresh blackberries over the dish before serving. Serve with something green.

UPSTAIRS DOWNSTAIRS FISH PIE

The name here derives from this fish dish's marriage of marine life from both ends of the social spectrum. From the mahogany dining table of the finest Belgravia mansion we have monkfish and some scallops; from the Whitechapel barrow of a kindly salt o' the earth type we have some cockles, all blended together like some Hollywood social experiment. The resulting pie, however, tastes nothing like any kind of experiment, and provides the perfect balance of fresh fishiness with roasted, browned topping – and no sign of the watery, mashed potato that nanny used to use in her fish pie.

◆ INGREDIENTS ◆

Serves 4

200ml double or single cream
 – whatever you have to
 hand
200ml sour cream
75ml white wine
juice and zest of ½ lemon
2 tablespoons soft herbs
 – any one or combination
 of flat-leaf parsley, dill,
 chervil, lovage, chives,
 chopped
200g monkfish, cut into
 2cm chunks
200g scallops, halved if
 large; aim for 2cm chunks
100g cockles
100g fresh or Panko
 breadcrumbs
100g sharp hard cheese,
 such as mature Cheddar
good grind of black
 pepper

(1) Preheat oven to 200°C/gas mark 6

(2) Mix the creams, wine, lemon and herbs together in a small saucepan and bring to the boil. Turn off the heat.

(3) Meanwhile, scatter the fish, scallops and cockles evenly in a baking dish – or individual ones. Pour over the cream mixture and a good grind of black pepper.

(4) Mix the breadcrumbs and cheese together in a small bowl, and sprinkle this mixture over the fish/cream.

(5) Bake for 10 minutes until the topping is a golden colour, and serve piping hot.

You can substitute half the cream for fish stock for a less rich option. Thickening the sauce is not necessary; it is lovely as it is. Any leftovers are delicious tipped into a hollowed-out baked potato, and warmed through in the oven. You can also happily reheat the dish.

SKATE WITH SORREL AND BROWN BUTTER

Skate is an ancient fish closely related to sharks. There are three important things you need to know about skate. First, it doesn't keep; as it ages, skate breaks down and leaks ammonia (some fish improve with age – Dover sole is one example). So buy it fresh and cook it on the same day. Second, skate has no bones, just cartilage, so it is ideal for those a little squeamish about fish bones getting stuck in their throats. Third, unlike sharks, skates don't bite. We specify unsalted butter in this recipe because salted butter burns a little more easily.

♦ INGREDIENTS ♦

Serves 1 – multiply at will

1 skate wing, skin and central
    cartilage removed by your
    fishmonger
25g unsalted butter – or even
    clarified, if you have some left
    over from the Chicken Liver
    Pâté on page 94
plenty of salt and freshly
    ground black pepper

For the sorrel butter
50g butter
a few sorrel leaves (if you can't
    find sorrel, substitute with
    young spinach leaves and a
    squeeze of lemon)

(1) Preheat oven to 200°C/gas mark 6.

(2) Rinse the skate and pat dry with kitchen paper. Melt the butter in a frying pan until hot. Add the skate and quickly fry on each side for a minute until golden.

(3) Transfer to a baking dish and bake for 5–7 minutes.

(4) Meanwhile, wipe out the frying pan, melt the oil and butter and continue to cook until nut brown – don't let it burn. Let your nose be your guide. Turn off the heat, add the sorrel, which will wilt, and season to taste.

(5) Transfer the skate to a serving dish, pour over the sorrel butter and serve.

THE INVISIBLE HOST

How many times have you been seated in a restaurant, tucking into your lunch or dinner with relish, when a waitress shimmers over to you and asks whether everything is alright? 'Mmmm', you mumble through a mouthful of food, wondering what was the point of that exchange. A dinner host/ess should be the precise opposite of that waitress – he or she should deliver piles of superlative food to the table in serving dishes, provide each guest with a warm plate, and let them get on with it. The only occasion when the guests will become aware of the host is when he clears away the plates, and this should be done as discreetly and briskly as possible.

CHAPTER 6
VEGETABLES

Since the disappearance of the butler from most houses, the serving of dinner has become fraught with almost as much confusion as the cooking of it. Nobody really knows what is correct and consequently guests put up with whatever conditions are forced on them at their host's table, probably picking up bad habits that they will pass on at the next dinner party of their own.

Vegetables should never, ever be placed on the plate before serving the main meal. If serving something with specific quantities, such as veal escalopes, then by all means serve them on the plate – but don't put anything else on that plate! It should be up to your guests how much of each vegetable they want to eat, not you. For a large dinner, arrange the vegetables in such a way that they don't need to be passed around the table, i.e. place them in several smaller dishes rather than one large one. The same goes for potatoes, gravy and any special sauces you are providing.

CHAP'S MASHED POTATOES

Mashed potato is endlessly versatile. You can liven it up by adding a mugful of frozen peas, a big bunch of chopped flat-leaf parsley or stirring in some grated cheese before serving. Some cookery writers make a fuss about floury versus waxy potatoes. The debate rages on: some people think floury are best but, because they are drier, they suck up more moisture and fat than the waxy sort. Since the potato aisle of a supermarket is not a particularly interesting place to lurk, we suggest grabbing a bag of pink-skinned potatoes, as they tend to be the most flavoursome, and swiftly moving on.

EQUIPMENT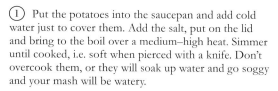

Masher and electric beater or
   sieve or ricer

◆ INGREDIENTS ◆

Serves 6

750g potatoes, peeled and
   cut into largish chunks
½ teaspoon salt
150ml milk or single or double
   cream
approx. 100g butter
scraping of nutmeg
plenty of salt and freshly
   ground black pepper

① Put the potatoes into the saucepan and add cold water just to cover them. Add the salt, put on the lid and bring to the boil over a medium–high heat. Simmer until cooked, i.e. soft when pierced with a knife. Don't overcook them, or they will soak up water and go soggy and your mash will be watery.

② Drain and return to the pan over a low heat. Pour in the milk or cream, butter and nutmeg and heat the liquid before you begin to mash. Mash the potatoes with a masher until smooth. Ideally, use an electric beater to finish it off and make it super-smooth or use a sieve or ricer. Taste and add salt and pepper to your liking. You may want to add more butter and milk or cream.

To make the dish more decorative, you may want to make the texture very soft (like whipped cream), and then pile into an ovenproof dish and bake at 180°C/gas mark 4 for 15 minutes to get a nice crust on top.

ROAST POTATOES

Few can resist roast potatoes – especially when cooked to crispy perfection. To judge how many potatoes you need, look at the size of your potatoes: a large potato can be cut into 4 or 6 pieces; 3 or 4 pieces per person is usually enough. Of course it is always a good idea to make a few extra, as roast potatoes are so delicious cold – just increase the quantities below.

◆ INGREDIENTS ◆

Serves 2

50g goose fat/beef dripping/
    oil/mixture of oil and
    butter
2 medium potatoes – peeled
    and cut into quarters
powdered mustard (optional)
plenty of sea salt and freshly
    ground black pepper

(1) Preheat the oven to 220°C/gas mark 7.

(2) Put the oil or fat in a large roasting tin and get it smoking hot in the oven. Meanwhile, put the potatoes into a saucepan and add salted water just to cover them. Bring to the boil and simmer for approx. 7–10 minutes. This is called par-boiling.

(3) Drain and return to the pan over a low heat to dry out. This bit is crucial for crispy potatoes: give them a good shake to release any trapped water or steam and to rough up the edges, which will help them crisp in the oven. This is also a good time to sprinkle liberally with sea salt and black pepper and even a bit of powdered mustard, if you like, as it will coat them nicely and stick to the outsides.

(4) Remove the roasting tin from the oven and tip in the potatoes. Using a large spoon/tongs, turn them over in the fat to coat them and spread them out evenly. Of course you could simply add them to a roasting tin with the meat, if you wish.

(5) Roast for 1 hour, shaking them occasionally to stop them sticking and to ensure that nothing is burning.

GRATED ROOT VEGETABLE CAKES

Grated Root Vegetable Cakes may sound a bit like something you'd find in a health food shop, should you have accidentally wandered into one. But don't worry – they are not particularly healthy, just incredibly colourful, crispy and bursting with a variety of earthy flavours.

EQUIPMENT

Individual muffin tins, a cake tin or a roasting tin

♦ INGREDIENTS ♦

Serves 2; multiply at will

25g oil mixed with 25g melted
    butter – olive or vegetable oil
    is fine, but you could also use
    walnut or pumpkin seed oil
400g root veg, e.g. carrots,
    potatoes, parsnip, beetroot,
    celeriac – peeled and finely
    grated
scraping of nutmeg
plenty of salt and freshly
    ground black pepper

(1) Preheat oven to 190°C/gas mark 5. Use a little of the fat to grease the sides and base of your chosen tin(s).

(2) Put the grated vegetables, oil, melted butter, nutmeg, salt and pepper into a large bowl. Mix well to combine evenly.

(3) Pack the vegetables into the tin(s) and press down. If you want to make individual vegetable cakes and don't have muffin tins, wet your hands, form the vegetable mixture into individual patties and arrange on a baking tray.

(4) Roast in the oven for 30 minutes. Halfway through cooking, press the cakes down again. They are ready when soft in the middle when pierced with a sharp knife, but crispy and crunchy and golden brown on top.

BRAISED BABY LETTUCES

Wait a minute, you cry – *hot* salad? Whoever heard of such a thing? Well, diners of the early twentieth century were extremely fond of cooking vegetables today associated with salad. So don't think of these side dishes as hot salads. Simply consider them a new way of treating what can be, let's face it, rather dull and tasteless vegetables.

EQUIPMENT

Small baking dish to fit 8 halves of lettuce snugly

♦ INGREDIENTS ♦

Serves 4

75g butter
4 Little Gem lettuces, halved lengthways
150ml white wine or chicken/vegetable stock or mixture of both
sea salt and freshly ground black pepper

(1) Preheat oven 180°C/gas mark 4. Butter the baking dish using 25g of the butter.

(2) Arrange the lettuces in the baking dish with the cut sides uppermost. Pour over the wine or stock, sprinkle with salt and pepper and dot with the remaining 50g butter. Cover with baking parchment and overlay with foil, crimping the sides to seal.

(3) Place the dish on a baking sheet in oven and braise for 30 minutes.

(4) Remove the 'lid' and serve at table – don't forget to spoon on the lovely juices.

HOT CUCUMBER IN CREAM

♦ INGREDIENTS ♦

Serves 4

30g butter
1 cucumber, peeled, cut lengthwise, deseeded and chopped into 3cm chunks
1 teaspoon mustard seeds (optional)
juice of ½ lemon
150ml whipping, double or clotted cream
small bunch soft herbs, such as dill, flat-leaf parsley or chervil, roughly chopped (optional)
salt and freshly ground black pepper

(1) Melt the butter in a frying pan, add the cucumbers (and the mustard seed, if using) and fry gently for 3–5 minutes. Add the lemon juice and let it bubble for a moment.

(2) Stir in the cream and let bubble and boil for 2 minutes. Check for seasoning, add salt and pepper to taste and the chopped soft herbs.

HONEY-BRAISED SHALLOTS

Do you remember that short-lived fad in the 1990s for glazed onion tarts? Silly, wasn't it? Well, this is a recipe that has been around for much longer than that, and with good reason. A shallot is already a delicious vegetable, often lost among other fried vegetables. Making a solo appearance, honey-glazed and served in generous quantities, shallots really come into their own and will doubtless receive the praise from your guests that they deserve.

♦ INGREDIENTS ♦

Serves 2

10 small shallots
50g butter
2 tablespoons runny honey
1 tablespoon wine or cider
    vinegar
1 teaspoon thyme – fresh or
    dried – or another hard herb
    if you have it, e.g. rosemary
plenty of salt and freshly
    ground black pepper

(1) Preheat oven to 190°C/gas mark 5.

(2) Peel the shallots. If yours are tricky to peel, try soaking them in boiling water for 1 minute. Drain and rinse under cold water. They should slip their skins easily. Keep them whole. Cut off the minimum amount of root – we want them to stay intact.

(3) Put them in a roasting tin with the butter, honey, vinegar, thyme and salt and pepper. Roast them for 40–50 minutes, turning every now and then in the sticky honey juices. They are ready when soft and easily pierced by a sharp knife.

DINNER GUEST ETIQUETTE

'Does anyone want this last delicious braised lettuce/artichoke heart/roast potato?' Thus does the refrain echo across countless dinner tables, with all the guests squirming in their seats with a mixture of salivating desire for said lone vegetable in the dish, and an awkward British guilt at being greedy enough to think 'I do!', never mind actually to say it. According to *The Young Man's Companion* (1895), an etiquette guide for gentlemen, it is the very refusal of the offer for the last vegetable that is the height of rudeness. In those days, etiquette was all about flattering your host and providing him with reassurances that he keeps both an excellent cellar and a first-class kitchen. So to turn down a vegetable would be considered an insult to the repast he has provided, with the implication that the meal was so mediocre that guests can't even finish it.

CABBAGE/SPRING GREENS VICHY STYLE

Both cabbage and spring greens are the sorts of vegetables that children refuse to eat – and they may have a point if they have been cooked traditionally, i.e. by over-boiling them. The Vichy style does not refer to annexing the vegetables during the Second World War, but to a French style of cookery using small amounts of water, butter and wine, resulting in crisp yet moist vegetables that even children will enjoy. Mari Simpson, honorary chap, enlightened Clare as to this method of cooking the green stuff and now she rarely uses any other method.

◆ INGREDIENTS ◆

Serves 2
1 cabbage, green or Savoy –
shredded or cut into small
pieces
50g butter
350ml mixture of water and
white wine (roughly half and
half, or whatever ratio
appeals to you)
a handful of fresh herbs
(optional), such as tarragon,
chervil, dill or flat-leaf
parsley, chopped
salt and freshly ground black
pepper

① Pile the cabbage into a large, wide saucepan. Add the butter, water, wine and salt and pepper. Put over a medium–high heat. Let the mixture bubble and steam away uncovered, stirring the cabbage occasionally.

② After about 10 minutes the liquid will be gone and the cabbage tender. Stir in the herbs and check for seasoning before serving.

PURÉED CARROTS

Uncle Monty in *Withnail & I* had nothing but praise for carrots: 'I think the carrot infinitely more fascinating than the geranium. The carrot has mystery. Flowers are essentially tarts. Prostitutes for the bees. There is, you'll agree, a certain *je ne sais quoi* oh so very special about a firm, young carrot.' He may have been offended by us pureeing his beloved carrots to a pulp, but served this way they can provide a welcome splash of bright colour to the table.

EQUIPMENT

Blender

♦ INGREDIENTS ♦

Serves 4-6

3 large carrots, peeled and
　chopped into coins or
　chunks or sticks
50g butter
juice of ½ lemon or orange
salt and white pepper

Optional extras
2–3 tablespoons double
　cream
glug of white wine
handful of fresh herbs

① Steam or boil the carrots until tender – approx. 10 minutes.

② Drain, reserving approx. 1 mugful of the liquid, and rinse the carrots under the cold tap until they are ice-cold all the way through. This will preserve their colour.

③ Put them in a blender with the butter, lemon or orange juice and a little of the liquid to help them purée. Taste, and adjust seasoning. You can add cream at this point if you like, or some wine, and/or a handful of chopped herbs to leave little green flecks and a delicious aroma. The purée will be bright orange and will keep its colour when reheated gently in a pan or in the microwave. It can be made a day or two in advance.

SLOW-FRIED CARROTS WITH SPICES

What is it about carrots that some of us just don't like? Is it the memory of school dinners, where the offensive disks of orange sat moodily on the plate defying anyone to enjoy them? Our method of slow frying carrots with spices adds a welcome dash of flavour to an otherwise insipid vegetable.

♦ INGREDIENTS

Serves 4–6

75g butter
6 large carrots, peeled and
　chopped
2 tablespoons caraway,
　onion or fennel mustard
　seeds – or a combination
salt and freshly ground black
　pepper

① Melt the butter in a frying pan over a medium–low heat, add the carrots and the spices. Stir around and gently sweat for 25 minutes. Taste, and adjust seasoning.

ROAST ARTICHOKE HEARTS

We got this recipe from Ian Fleming's *Casino Royale*, in which James Bond consumes some beef tournedos served with a single artichoke heart, in an uncharacteristically modest serving. We've scaled it up to four or five artichoke hearts. We suggest you use artichokes from a can rather than peeling fresh ones yourself.

♦ I N G R E D I E N T S ♦

Serves 1 – multiply at will

4–5 artichoke hearts – tinned
   ones are fine
1 tablespoon chopped fresh
   thyme (or use dried)
1 tablespoon lemon juice
2 tablespoons olive oil
plenty of salt and freshly
   ground black pepper

① Preheat oven to 200°C/gas mark 6.

② Drain the artichoke hearts, if canned, and place in a baking dish.

③ Chuck in the thyme and then add the lemon juice, olive oil and salt and pepper.

④ Transfer to the oven and cook for 10 minutes.

— CHAPTER 7 —

SUPPER

'The tears were hardly dry on my cheeks after Noel Coward's *Cavalcade* when we got to supper at the Savoy and were regaled with a wonderful *soupe à l'oignon*.' How many of us can say that, as Constance Spry did in *Hostess* (1961)? It's an excellent example of the role supper used to play in people's lives, and how important it is that we re-introduce it. In a modern context, supper makes perfect sense: how many British social occasions, occurring in the early part of the evening, have left you returning home with a rumbling tummy? (Naturally, you will have walked past the queues outside fast-food outlets with a shudder.) Supper, a light meal taken anywhere between 9pm and midnight, takes you gently into slumber without overfilling you and giving you nightmares.

BAKED EGGS
WITH SPINACH AND MUSHROOMS

✕

❝ Baked eggs? Really?', we hear you cry. Surely some things are retro in a bad way, like a Reliant Robin rather than a Classic Bentley? Yes they are, but baked eggs is one of those meals, like many in this book, which disappeared by accident rather than design. Somehow, eggs migrated to the breakfast menu and stayed there, occasionally getting a look-in at lunch as an omelette or, hard-boiled, as picnic fare. Eggs are far too good to leave behind in the morning and provide a pleasantly fortifying bit of protein late in the evening, without the need for any kind of meat. You can use any green leafy vegetable, such as chard or kale, but our secret ingredient, if pushed for time, is frozen leaf spinach (but absolutely not the chopped variety).

◆ INGREDIENTS ◆

Serves 1 – multiply at will

knob of butter
2 balls frozen leaf spinach
5 mushrooms, whole, halved
   or sliced
drizzle of wine dregs, if
   handy
2 tablespoons slivered
   leftover meat or fish – or
   cockles work very well
2 eggs

(1) Preheat oven to 190°C/gas mark 5.

(2) Put a knob of butter in the bottom of a baking dish – for flavour. Chuck in the frozen spinach, mushrooms, wine (if using), meat, etc. (if using).

(3) Crack in your eggs and season generously. Cover lightly with a sheet of foil and bake for 12 minutes.

SMOKED HADDOCK
BAKED IN CREAM

Why try to be a clever chap with a fish as tasty as smoked haddock? Whichever salt o' the earth fellow in Grimsby took the trouble of smoking your haddock has done most of the work in bringing out its good points, so all you need to do is serve it in a manner that draws attention to, rather than obliterates, its succulent flavour. The result is a warming, filling meal for a cold winter's eve, ideally served with a flagon of real ale.

◆ INGREDIENTS ◆

Serves 2

1 piece, approx. 200g, undyed
   smoked haddock fillet,
   skinned
150ml single cream
pinch of mace
generous grind of white
   pepper
½ lemon, for squeezing
   (optional)
crusty bread, to serve
Braised Baby Lettuces, to serve

(1) Preheat oven to 200°C/gas mark 6.

(2) Place the fillet in a nice baking dish in which it just fits. Pour over the cream and add the mace and white pepper. Transfer to the oven and bake for 15 minutes – check the centre of the fish to ensure it is flaky, which means it is cooked. If you are a fan of lemon you can squeeze over some juice.

(3) Ideally serve this in its baking dish with some crusty bread and Braised Baby Lettuces (see page 118).

CHICKEN LIVERS
IN REDCURRANT JELLY

Chicken is so commonplace these days, and in such varying quality, that it barely makes the grade as a meat any more; it has almost been reduced to the rank of a mere cheese or a vegetable. Chicken livers are the exception; the neglected portion of this reliable fowl are its dark secret, one it often takes to the grave, the rest of it having been turned into something smothered in breadcrumbs and served in a bucket. In our recipe, the deep savoury flavour of the chicken livers is balanced nicely by the sweetness of the redcurrants. By all means throw in a handful of fresh redcurrants if you have some. Serve with vegetables, salad or Melba toast (see page 24).

◆ INGREDIENTS ◆

Serves 1 – multiply at will

3 or 4 chicken livers – organic
    are best, for obvious reasons
pinch of mace
30g butter
garlic or shallot, finely
    chopped (optional)
2 tablespoons redcurrant
    sauce or jelly
salt and freshly ground black
    pepper
vegetables, salad or Melba toast,
    to serve

(1) Halve the chicken livers and snip out the cores using sharp scissors. Rinse and pat dry with kitchen paper. Sprinkle with a little mace, salt and pepper.

(2) Melt the butter in a frying pan, toss in the livers and fry over a medium heat for approx. 3 minutes on each side if you like them slightly pink in the centre; cook them a little longer if you like them well done. Remove using a slotted spoon and put them on a warm plate. (If you are very fond of garlic and shallots, you could add some to the pan, finely chopped, and fry in the butter for a couple of minutes before adding the livers.)

(3) Turn up the heat and add the redcurrant sauce or jelly to the pan, stir around to pick up all the lovely flavours and pour over the livers. Serve.

 NOTE: You are already halfway to a pâté with this recipe! Purée this in a blender with a little cream, pile into little pots and chill, and you have a superb pâté.

LOVE APPLES
STUFFED WITH CRAB

Have you noticed how tomatoes have got smaller and smaller over the years, with every passing fad for Tuscan this and Tunisian that? If this carries on, tomatoes will end up being overshadowed by the capers in salads. We reserve the right to reclaim the humble beefsteak tomato from its dejected place as a 1970s throwback. Seductively red-skinned and sweet-fleshed, the tomato wasn't called the 'love apple' for nothing. Stuffed with crab, whose salty, fishy flavour blends harmoniously with the zesty, earthy flavours of the other ingredients, this dish can be made the previous night so that the taste develops, making it an ideal dish to serve a large group of guests. You can also make smaller versions with normal-sized tomatoes; it's just a tad more fiddly.

EQUIPMENT

Melon baller (optional)

♦ INGREDIENTS ♦

Serves 1 – multiply at will

1 beefsteak tomato
100g crabmeat, white or dark
    meat or a mixture
1 spring onion, finely
    chopped
½ anchovy fillet, roughly
    chopped (optional)
zest and juice of ¼ lemon
2 stems dill, finely chopped
6cm cucumber, peeled,
    seeded and diced
1 small gherkin, chopped
    (optional)
2 radishes, chopped
5cm piece of fennel,
    chopped (optional)
pinch of cayenne
sprinkle of salt and freshly
    ground black pepper
Melba toast, to serve

(1) Cut a tiny sliver off the base of the tomatoes, if necessary, to ensure they stand up. Cut down around the stalk to remove it, making a hole approx. 5cm diameter. Using a teaspoon or melon baller, scoop out the seeds and put them into a sieve balanced over a bowl, to collect the juice.

(2) Mix the crabmeat, spring onion, anchovy (if using), lemon zest and juice, dill, cucumber, gherkin (if using), radishes, fennel (if using) and cayenne in a bowl. Season with salt and pepper, mix in the reserved tomato juice (discard the seeds) and pile the mixture into the tomato. Serve with Melba toast (see page 24).

BUTLER BRAIN FOOD

For centuries, herrings were the staple fish of this nation, being fished by the trawler-load and providing chaps with their kippers. For some inexplicable reason they have fallen out of favour, replaced in restaurants by fish with fancier sounding names such as Sea Bream and Red Snapper, despite the fact that herrings are particularly high in those coveted omega-3 fatty acids. This dish uses the herring roe, a particularly soft and succulent roe, to create a dish that is not only delicious but will also engorge the brain to Jeeves-like proportions.

♦ INGREDIENTS ♦

Serves 1 – multiply at will

3 soft herring roes
4 tablespoons oatmeal,
    seasoned with a little salt and
    pepper and cayenne if liked
50g butter
50ml mayonnaise or cream –
    any type you have handy
2 teaspoons chopped capers
    or gherkins
½ teaspoon horseradish
freshly ground black pepper
    and a little salt, to taste
toast, salad or vegetables, to serve

① Rinse the roes. Pat dry. Roll in seasoned oatmeal.

② Melt the butter in a frying pan. Add the roes and fry gently. When the underside is golden and crisp, turn over and fry the other side – approx. 8 minutes in total. Remove and drain excess fat on kitchen paper. The roes will keep warm in a low oven for approx. 20 minutes if necessary.

③ Meanwhile, mix the mayo/cream, capers/gherkins and horseradish to make a sauce. Taste to ensure it is seasoned correctly.

④ Serve the roes on a warm plate with sauce. Delicious with buttered toast or vegetables or salad. This dish also makes a very good first course.

CAVALRY PÂTÉ MUSHROOMS

How many times have you lunged at the fridge at midnight in search of an appetising snack, only to find, along with the obligatory bottle of champagne, a modest selection of seemingly disparate ingredients that no amount of imagination can concoct into a full meal? A punnet of mushrooms, a jar of mustard and a large wedge of country pâté, for example? Here is a recipe that blends precisely those ingredients into a full, hearty and, if one may say so, rather impressive dish to serve at the midnight table.

♦ INGREDIENTS ♦

Serves 1 – multiply at will

1 horse or field mushroom
100g (or more) pâté – your
    favourite sort
50g breadcrumbs
15g butter, melted – or you
    could use 1 tablespoon nut
    oil, e.g. walnut or hazelnut,
    plus extra for greasing
½ teaspoon made mustard –
    your favourite sort
a sprinkling of dried or fresh
    herbs (optional), e.g. thyme,
    flat-leaf parsley, rosemary or
    lovage, finely chopped

(1) Preheat oven to 180°C/gas mark 4.

(2) Wipe over the mushroom, trim the stalk, peel if you feel it is necessary. If your pâté is soft, spread it over the gills of the mushroom. If your pâté is firm, cut it into slices and arrange over the gills of the mushroom.

(3) Mix together the breadcrumbs, melted butter, mustard and – if you are using them – herbs. Sprinkle this over the pâté. Butter or oil a baking dish, put in the mushroom and bake for 25 minutes until the breadcrumbs are golden and the mushroom is dark and tender.

DEVILLED MACKEREL WITH BEETROOT

Mackerel, another neglected denizen of the sea, is so oily that you won't need to apply any brilliantine to your hair after devouring this dish. We have already advocated the devilling process in this book due to the fact that, before food from the Indian subcontinent became popular in this country, food was only ever served in two ways: plain or devilled. The plain variety was still full of flavour, but the devilling process added that extra kick that some gentlemen feel they need late in the evening.

♦ I N G R E D I E N T S ♦

Serves 1 hungry person

1 tablespoon Worcestershire sauce
1 tablespoon mustard powder
2 mackerel fillets – briney fresh!
1 small beetroot, peeled (if you don't like raw, use ready-cooked vacuum-packed; if you don't like beetroot, use a carrot)
small piece of celeriac, peeled
1 spring onion, sliced
3 pickled walnuts, quartered, or chopped finer if liked
1 tablespoon any good oil, e.g. rapeseed, hazelnut or groundnut, etc.
1 teaspoon lemon juice or wine, sherry or cider vinegar:
salt and freshly ground black pepper

1. Preheat grill to hot or oven to 200°C/gas mark 6.

2. Mix together the Worcestershire sauce and mustard powder on a plate. Slash the skin of the mackerel twice to stop the fish curling up when cooked. Dip the mackerel fillets in the devilling sauce.

3. Put under the grill, skin side uppermost, and cook for approx. 3 minutes on each side. If using the oven, put in a baking tin, skin side uppermost, and cook for 7–10 minutes.

4. Meanwhile, finely grate the beetroot and celeriac into a bowl. Stir in the spring onion. Add the pickled walnuts. Pour over the oil, lemon juice/vinegar and salt and pepper and mix together.

5. Pile the beetroot salad on a plate and served topped with the devilled mackerel fillets.

SWEETBREADS

❝ Sweetbreads' is the polite word for various portions of a calf or lamb's throat, gullet and neck. The name came from seventeenth-century cooks who, along with calling sheep's intestines 'chitterlings', had no intention of masking grotesque foodstuffs with cute names; they simply wanted to spend less time explaining themselves to the butcher. Sadly, times have changed and there is a certain contemporary squeamishness at eating the inside, rather than the outside, of animals. Perhaps best to explain all this to your guests before serving them such an innocent-sounding portion. Or even better, let them enjoy the delicious flavour and then tell them afterwards.

♦ INGREDIENTS ♦

Serves 1 – multiply at will

4 lambs' sweetbreads
a little plain flour seasoned
    with salt and pepper, for
    dipping
50g butter
1 rasher of bacon (any sort),
    sliced small
4 sage leaves
splash of booze, any sort of
    cream or stock (optional)
salt and freshly ground black
    pepper

① Sweetbreads are easier to prepare if first you soak them in cold water for an hour. If you are not cooking immediately, you can change the water and leave them in the fridge until you need them.

② To cook, put the sweetbreads in a pan of cold water, bring to the boil and boil for 1 minute. Drain and refresh under cold water – this stops them cooking any further and they will be cool enough to handle. Now you can peel off the membrane and trim any loose bits. This is the way cooks have prepared sweetbreads for the last 300 years and there is no reason to change it.

③ Slice the sweetbreads in half, and then dry them with kitchen paper. Dip in the seasoned flour and tap off the excess.

④ Heat the butter in a frying pan, add the bacon and sage and fry for a few minutes until golden – or however you prefer your bacon. Add the sweetbreads, sprinkle with a little salt and pepper and fry on each side for about 4 minutes until crisp and golden.

⑤ At this point they are cooked and ready to serve. If you like, you can splash in a little alcohol such as brandy or sherry, or add a little cream or stock to create a bit more of a sauce.

ENGLISH RABBIT

Not to be confused with Welsh Rarebit, an equally delicious recipe well documented elsewhere. The English version, in keeping with our national habits, contains more booze and eyebrow-raising cheese, and is more than something for old ladies to nibble on in provincial tearooms. English Rabbit is more suited to a chap just back from the opera, feeling somewhat emotionally drained after a viewing of *La Traviata* and in need of something fortifying and tasty that will wash down nicely with a glass or twain of Claret. We have adapted this recipe from Elizabeth Ayrton's *The Cookery of England* (1830) – however, her version rather racily soaks the bread in wine first. You could seek out a copy and try it for yourself.

◆ I N G R E D I E N T S ◆

Serves 1 – multiply at will

1 thin slice of bread
1 glass plus 1 tablespoon red
   wine or port
30g butter
100g cheese, grated or crumbled
   (any strong English cheese –
   Stilton is nice)
1 teaspoon made English
   mustard

(1) Preheat grill.

(2) Drizzle the bread with approx. 1 tablespoon of the red wine or port. Dot with half of the butter and put it under the grill, turning once.

(3) Put the remaining butter and wine or port in a saucepan along with the cheese and mustard and place over a moderate heat for 2–3 minutes, stirring until it is smoothly mixed. Spread it quickly on the toasted bread and return to the grill to brown. Serve immediately.

LEEKS IN BREEKS

The leek is a noble example of British vegetation oft overlooked, due to its tendency to become rather soggy when boiled and look a bit on the limp side. This recipe, however, raises the poor blighter higher in the ranks by cladding him in livery made from a succulent chunk of ham. Serve in the officer's mess or elsewhere, with a favourite chutney or some Worcestershire sauce. Crusty bread is also a delicious accompaniment. You don't have to be Welsh to enjoy this, but it does help.

♦ INGREDIENTS ♦

Serves 2 – multiply at will

2 leeks, white parts only, cut
    in half to make two short
    pieces
2 slices good-quality ham,
    halved
150ml single cream
6 tablespoons white wine
2 teaspoons made English
    mustard – or to taste
½ teaspoon mace
100g mature cheese, grated
salt and freshly ground black
    pepper

(1) Preheat oven to 190°C/gas mark 5.

(2) Bring a saucepan of water to the boil and plunge in the leeks. Cook for 5 minutes. Drain, squeezing them a little to ensure no water is trapped. Wrap each leek in a piece of ham and place in a baking dish.

(3) Mix together the cream, white wine, mustard, mace and half the grated cheese. Season with salt and pepper and then pour over the leeks. Sprinkle over the remaining cheese and bake in the oven for 30 minutes. The leeks will be tender and flavourful and the sauce bubbling.

SLIVERS OF LIVER AND BACON

If the entertainment from which you've just returned didn't involve large ladies singing beautiful arias, but energetic thespians throwing furniture around the stage, you may need something with a bit of kick to bring your mind back to earthly concerns. Slivers of Liver and Bacon will do just that. They are delicious served with our Cabbage Vichy (page 121) or Puréed Carrots (page 122).

EQUIPMENT

Cocktail sticks or skewers

◆ I N G R E D I E N T S ◆

Serves 1 – multiply at will

50g fresh breadcrumbs
small bunch of fresh flat-leaf
  parsley, chopped
zest and juice of ½ lemon
45g butter, melted
approx. 6 peeled chestnuts,
  chopped
1 tablespoon sherry
3 slices of smoked streaky
  bacon, cut in half
2 lambs' livers, cut in 3 thin
  horizontal slices

(1) Preheat oven to 180°C/gas mark 4.

(2) For the filling: mix the breadcrumbs, flat-leaf parsley, lemon zest and juice, melted butter, chopped chestnuts and sherry together in a bowl.

(3) Stretch each rasher of bacon with the back of a knife, 'spreading' it like butter to lengthen.

(4) Lay a slice of liver on each slice of bacon. Top with the crumbs and roll up, securing with a cocktail stick or skewer. Put them all in a baking dish, fitting snugly, and bake for 15 minutes. Alternatively, fry in a knob of butter, turning to cook on all sides, for 12–15 minutes.

CHAPTER 8

PUDDINGS &
SAVOURIES

There is an exclusive club deep in the Cotswolds called the Pudding Club, where they serve nothing but puddings for the entire sitting, the guests emerging high on sugar and bursting out of their trousers. No country other than Britain could have this, for, while we are perhaps not world renowned for our cuisine, our puddings are certainly the stuff of legend. We are probably the only country in the world whose more traditional restaurants maintain a dedicated fleet of trolleys specifically deployed for the delivery of puddings to the table.

WHIM WHAM

The famous British trifle has also been known, since as early as 1660, as a whim wham or a foole. The basis was always some form of biscuit or cake, soaked in alcohol, then layered with anything from jam to custard. The beauty of a trifle is that not only does it use up all the leftover dribs and drabs in your cocktail cabinet, but it can, if you wish, pack such a punch that your guests will remember it for its intoxicating, as well as flavoursome, qualities.

◆ INGREDIENTS ◆

Serves 8

approx. 8 sponge finger or
   ratafia biscuits (or use amaretti
   biscuits) – if you prefer sponge
   cake, use that
4 tablespoons Marsala wine
450g your favourite soft fruit –
   raspberries, any berries,
   bananas, slices of plum or
   peach or nectarines or oranges
2 tablespoons elderflower
   cordial
2 tablespoons sloe gin (or just
   gin if you're a fast drinker!)
4 tablespoons advocaat
½ quantity Custard (see page
   165) made with single cream
   instead of milk (or use approx.
   300ml ready-made custard)
300ml double cream
2 tablespoons icing sugar
3 tablespoons vanilla vodka –
   or vodka with ½ teaspoon
   vanilla extract

To decorate (optional)
Anything you like to sprinkle
   on top, e.g. flaked almonds,
   raspberries, blueberries, fresh lemon
   or orange zest or seeds from a couple
   of vanilla pods

EQUIPMENT

Pretty 1 litre bowl or dish – preferably glass – or you can make individual ones in glasses. Once you have all the elements prepared, you can see how big your glasses will need to be.

....

(1) Arrange the sponge finger biscuits in the base of a large bowl. Drizzle with the Marsala wine.

(2) Break up your chosen fruit a little so the juices start to ooze and the booze can be soaked up. Stir the fruit around in a bowl with the elderflower cordial and sloe gin to get the juices going. Now tip this on to the sponge fingers.

(3) Stir the advocaat into the custard and pour on top of the fruit.

(4) Whip the cream with the icing sugar and vanilla vodka until it forms soft, flopping peaks. Stop beating immediately. Don't overwhip! Pour this lovely concoction over the rest as a final layer.

(5) To finish, sprinkle with your chosen decorative touches – or get artistic and make a pattern out of berries.

Note: Trifle is always best if made at least 4 hours before eating – and preferably a day ahead – to allow the flavours to soak and meld. It keeps jolly well for a couple of days after serving, too.

SUSSEX POND PUDDING

This traditional recipe dates back to sixteenth-century Sussex and originally it would have been boiled in a portion of animal gut. This was later replaced by a cloth and this method of cooking the pudding lasted well until the 1930s. The 'pond' refers to the delicious lemony, buttery sauce that oozes out when you slice the pudding open. You can cook yours in a piece of animal intestine if you like, but the resulting flavour will be much the same as using our slightly more modern method.

EQUIPMENT

1.5 litre pudding basin – easiest if you have a plastic one with a lid, but if not you can use baking parchment and string
Large, lidded saucepan, big enough to accommodate the pudding basin

◆ INGREDIENTS ◆

Serves 6

250g self-raising flour
125g suet
¼ teaspoon salt
75ml milk
250g unsalted butter, cut into little cubes
250g light brown sugar
1 unwaxed lemon, washed and pricked all over with a sharp knife

① To make the suet pastry: mix the flour, suet and salt in a large bowl or food-processor. Make a well in the centre, add the milk and 75ml water, and then mix to bind into a soft dough – not too sticky and not dry. It needs to be rollable.

② Put the dough on a lightly floured surface and cut out a quarter (this will form the lid). Roll out the remainder into a circle large enough to line the base and sides of your pudding basin.

③ Put half the cubed butter and half the sugar in the base, then the whole lemon and then the remainder of the butter and sugar.

④ Roll out the spare pastry into a disc large enough to fit as a lid, put it on top and press the pastry edges together to form a nice seal.

⑤ If you are using a plastic pudding basin with a lid, you don't need to do the next bit. Tear off a sheet of baking parchment wide enough to cover the top of the pudding with a generous 5cm pleat in the centre. This will allow the steam to expand it. Tie string around to hold the paper in place.

⑥ Put the basin into a large saucepan and pour boiling water around the basin to come halfway up the sides. Put the saucepan lid on and simmer over a low-medium heat for 3 hours. Check periodically and add extra boiling water if the level gets low.

⑦ When it is ready, lift the basin out of the saucepan and remove the paper or lid. Dry the basin. Loosen the pudding around the sides with a palette knife, put a large dish on the top and quickly invert, shaking the pudding free.

⑧ Serve at table with custard, cream or ice cream.

SHIRT-SLEEVE PUDDING

First showcased by the great Mrs Beeton as Roly-Poly Pudding, this pudding also goes by the curious moniker of Dead Man's Arm or Dead Man's Leg – explained by the fact that it is cooked in an old shirt sleeve, thereby also collecting the title of Shirt-Sleeve Pudding. You can use any old shirt you like – and chaps know that that means pure cotton – but naturally your guests will shudder if it doesn't have French cuffs and isn't from Jermyn Street. Jam Roly Poly, for what it's worth, recently made the list of great British icons, voted for by the public, which included things like James Bond and red telephone booths.

EQUIPMENT

A shirt sleeve – if steaming – plus roasting tin and trivet and foil (or you can improvise with a piece of clean muslin or a clean tea towel)
String

◆ INGREDIENTS ◆

Serves 6

225g self-raising flour, plus a little extra for dusting
125g suet
pinch of salt
75g caster sugar, for rolling
225g blackberry jam
a handful of blackberries, fresh or frozen, plus extra to serve
Demerara or icing sugar, for dusting
Custard (page 165), to serve

1. Preheat oven to 200°C/gas mark 6.

2. To make the suet pastry: simply measure the flour, suet and salt into a large mixing bowl or food processor and stir to mix the ingredients evenly. Make a well in the centre and pour in 100–125ml water. Mix with a table knife to bind, until it comes away from the sides of the bowl. If it's too dry, add a little more water.

3. Turn it out and knead (lightly) on a lightly floured surface until soft and free from cracks.

4. Place a long sheet of baking parchment on a surface and sprinkle lightly but evenly with caster sugar. This will stop the pastry from sticking and make it easier to roll up. Place the dough onto this and roll into a rectangle approx. 5mm thick.

5. To make the pudding: warm the jam in a saucepan until it melts, making it easier to spread evenly, and spread over the surface of the pastry. Sprinkle over the blackberries. Fold over the edges about 1cm in – this forms a dam, stopping the jam escaping during cooking.

6. Starting with the short end nearest to you, begin to roll it up, lifting the parchment beneath up and over to do the rolling – you will end up with a neat rolled-up jam roly poly.

7. Insert the pudding into the shirtsleeve and tie up the ends with string. Put this onto the trivet in the roasting tin, fill up the roasting tin with hot water and tent the whole thing in foil. Place in the oven and steam for 45 minutes.

8. To serve, cut away the shirt-sleeve and dust the pudding with Demerara or icing sugar. Serve with custard and a few more blackberries.

Note: If inserting puddings into shirt sleeves and steaming them seems too much trouble, you may prefer to simply bake your pudding. To do this, at the end of step 6, slide the parchment paper and pudding on to a baking sheet and bake in the preheated oven for 30 minutes.

CLOOTIE DUMPLING

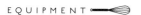

'Ne'er cast a cloot til Mey's oot' is something most of us are wont to say when winter still maintains its icy grip on our wardrobes. The saying counsels chaps not to be too hasty in the transition from tweed to linen, during the unpredictable build-up to the British summer. 'Cloot' was the Scots name for a piece of cloth, and its diminutive gave its name to this pudding, which is traditionally cooked in a piece of muslin or an old tea-towel.

EQUIPMENT

Large clean tea-towel, muslin
   or pure cotton fabric
String

INGREDIENTS

Serves 8–10

350g self-raising flour, plus extra
   for dredging
100g light brown sugar, plus
   extra for dredging
1 teaspoon cinnamon
1 teaspoon powdered ginger
450g sultanas
225g raisins
175g unsalted butter
1 tablespoon treacle
1 tablespoon golden syrup
2 eggs, beaten
100ml milk, plus extra if needed
Custard (page 165), to serve

(1) Put a large saucepan of water on to boil.

(2) Measure all the dry ingredients into a large mixing bowl or food-processor and stir to mix evenly. Rub in the butter. Make a well in the centre and pour in the wet ingredients. Stir to make a stiff mixture. You may need to add a little more milk. Form into a cannonball shape.

(3) Spread out the tea-towel and dredge with flour and sugar. Put the cannonball-shaped dumpling in the centre of the tea-towel and gather up the edges – not too tightly as it will expand as it cooks – and tie up the top with string. Lower the dumpling into a pan of boiling water, put on the lid, and simmer for 3 hours. Check periodically and add extra boiling water if the level gets low.

(4) To serve, unwrap the dumpling and put it on a lovely serving dish. Cut slices or wedges of dumpling and serve with Custard.

Leftover Clootie Dumpling is as good as fresh: fry thick slices in butter and sprinkle with sugar and cinnamon. This makes a very restorative breakfast for those who have enjoyed too much of the Scottish national drink the previous night, or those who are fortifying themselves for a bracing day of stalking or shooting.

BAKED CUSTARD POTS

Baked custard the French way has somehow ended up gracing practically every restaurant menu in the country under the title of Crème Brûlée, which not only has far too many accents for its own good, but means 'burnt custard'. As we all know, it is rare to get a good one these days, so we suggest going right back to before the crème brûlée epoch (1980s–2010s) and reviving the baked custard epoch (1920s onwards). Baked custard is a far more civilised, less French and altogether more predictable pudding – none of that hacking into a glassy burnt surface, only to find more hard custard underneath.

EQUIPMENT

4 little ramekins or pots, tea cups, etc.
Baking dish to hold the ramekins fairly snugly

◆ INGREDIENTS ◆

Serves 4

1 egg yolk and 1 whole egg
125g caster sugar
300ml single cream
½ teaspoon vanilla extract or scraping of nutmeg or pinch of cinnamon

① Preheat oven to 160°C/gas mark 3.

② Beat the whole egg, egg yolk and sugar well, add the cream and aromatics and beat again to mix.

③ Strain through a sieve into a jug – this will ensure a silky smooth custard and no air bubbles.

④ Set the ramekins into the baking dish and pour the custard mixture into them. Pour hot water into the baking dish to come halfway up the sides of the pots.

⑤ Bake in the oven for 30 minutes until just set.

⑥ Serve hot, warm or chilled. You can present the custards in their pots or turn them out when cool – run a knife around and invert onto a plate.

Strawberries are particularly good with this. Halve some strawberries, drizzle over a little elderflower cordial, stir and leave to infuse for 30 minutes to a couple of days. If leaving for longer than a couple of hours, refrigerate, but bring to room temperature before serving.

SYLLABUB

In Tudor times, Syllabub was created by milking a cow straight into a bucket containing some wine, cider or sherry. Or so they say. Sometimes it comes across as if the Tudors simply wanted everyone in the future to think of them as a bit peculiar. That said, this is one of their unique pudding legacies (along with gingerbread) that is really worth reviving, and indeed has become rather trendy in Britain in the last couple of years – but don't let that put you off. This is a good light pudding, best served after a heavy main course and perhaps before a selection of cheeses.

◆ INGREDIENTS ◆

Serves 2

2 tablespoons wine/
   sherry, etc
2 tablespoons caster sugar
75ml double or whipping
   cream
a little lemon zest or a
   scraping of nutmeg
   (optional)
biscuits, to serve

(1) Combine the ingredients in a large bowl, and whisk into a froth of soft peaks.

(2) Pile into glasses or nice dishes and serve.

Syllabub keeps well in the fridge for a couple of days. It is good served with biscuits.

BREAD, BUTTER AND LEMON CURD PUDDING

Nothing wrong with bread and butter pudding, but do we really need all those frazzled raisins littering it up like spent buckshot? Far better to use lemon curd instead, which adds a bright citrus dimension to this classic pudding. Please don't think you can get away with using sliced white bread, which you shouldn't have in the kitchen anyway. Some leftover white loaf from the bakers, or even brioche, will impart a far livelier flavour and it doesn't matter a hoot if it's slightly stale. Be as generous as you like with the lemon curd.

EQUIPMENT

Baking dish (about 750ml in capactiy)

♦ INGREDIENTS ♦

Serves 4–6

8 slices good-quality white bread from a proper loaf
50g unsalted butter
120g lemon curd
375ml single cream (or a mixture of cream and milk)
3 egg yolks
100g sugar – any sort, except dark brown or muscovado
1 teaspoon vanilla extract
¼ teaspoon salt

① Preheat oven to 170°C/gas mark 3.

② Make lemon curd sandwiches with the slices of bread, butter and lemon curd. You may cut off the crusts if you wish. Arrange the sandwiches, overlapping, in the dish, in as many layers as it takes, until it's all used up.

③ Now make the custard mixture by heating the cream in a saucepan. Meanwhile, in a heatproof bowl, beat the yolks with 50g of the sugar, vanilla and salt. Pour the hot cream onto the yolk/sugar mixture and whisk to combine thoroughly. Pour this mixture evenly over the lemon curd sandwiches in their dish and sprinkle with the remaining 50g sugar. Put the dish in a roasting tin or a tin that it will fit into easily, and pour in boiling water to come halfway up the sides.

④ Bake for 40 minutes. The custard will be soft but the top will be crunchy.

This is very nice served with some lovely stewed or fresh fruit from the garden.

TREACLE TART

In the film version of *Chitty Chitty Bang Bang*, that less chappish but equally impressive tome from the great Ian Fleming, the offer of free treacle tarts is precisely what the child-catcher uses to lure poor little Jeremy from the basement. Adults too will find this classic English pudding irresistible; you may find it is the magic ingredient that lures your guests to your house for dinner. This treacle tart is also an excellent way to use up that packet of Rich Tea biscuits that your aunt left behind, and that have no other practical use.

EQUIPMENT

Approx. 18cm tart tin or pie dish
Food processor – or large freezer bag and rolling pin

◆ INGREDIENTS ◆

Serves 6

200g unsalted butter
200g Rich Tea biscuits
500g golden syrup
100g treacle
zest and juice of 1 orange or lemon (optional)
185g fresh breadcrumbs
a pinch of salt

① Preheat oven to 180°C/gas mark 4.

② Melt the butter in a medium saucepan. Reduce the biscuits to fine crumbs in a food-processor or in a freezer bag with a rolling pin.

③ Tip the biscuits into the saucepan and stir around to coat in butter. Tip the mixture into a tart tin or pie dish and press evenly around the sides and bottom to form a base.

④ Put the golden syrup, treacle and pinch of salt into a saucepan and melt over a medium heat. Stir in the zest and juice of the orange or lemon (if using). Tip in the breadcrumbs and stir to mix evenly.

⑤ Pour the mixture over the biscuit base. Transfer to the oven and bake for 20–25 minutes.

RICE PUDDING
Thrice

Rice pudding occurs frequently in English literature, often paired with boiled mutton as an example of turgid, repetitive fare. However, further afield it is viewed as a pick-me-up for weary souls and even gets a reference in the story of the Buddha, who was apparently served rice pudding just before his enlightenment. Our three recipes will hopefully cover all eventualities and may possibly even lead to a sweet-toothed nirvana. Served hot, rice pudding is warming and comforting and invalids can eat much more of it than they could a savoury dish. It is also delicious served cold, with a sprinkling of sugar and cinnamon. Choose between the stovetop and oven versions, depending on how much time you have.

♦ INGREDIENTS ♦

Serves 4

45g pudding or Arborio rice
500ml full-fat milk
pinch of salt
3 tablespoons white
    sugar
scraping of nutmeg, or
    cinnamon stick or small
    piece of lemon peel
    (optional)

(1) Put the rice into a saucepan and just cover with water. Bring to the boil and drain through a sieve.

(2) If using the stove-top method: tip the rice into a saucepan with the milk, salt, sugar and whatever flavourings you prefer. Put over a low heat and cook without a lid, stirring gently regularly. It is done after about 20 minutes when it is glossy and thick.

(3) For the two oven versions (both end up with a skin): rinse out the pan, tip the rice back into the pan, add the milk, salt, sugar and your chosen flavouring, and then stir to combine. Pour this into a baking dish and bake at 180°C/gas mark 4 for 40 minutes or, for the really slow version, bake at 120°C/gas mark ½ for 6 hours, or overnight at 100°C/gas mark ¼.

FRUIT SOUP

Fruit soup may sound as unlikely as a cauliflower sandwich, but is fairly common in Scandinavian countries where, as we know, everything tends to be topsy-turvy. The choice of the fruit will affect the colour, so choose wisely. Stick to one type of soft fruit, e.g., berries, citrus fruits or melon. The resulting soup should always be perfectly smooth, chilled and delicately flavoured, somewhere between a pudding and a savoury. It can be served with biscuits or even a scoop of ice cream.

EQUIPMENT

Blender

♦ INGREDIENTS ♦

Serves 6

800g soft fruit (if using fruit
    with peel, this should be
    the peeled weight)
icing sugar, to taste
squeeze of lemon juice,
    to taste
splash of white wine or
    water, to taste
fresh herbs such as basil,
    lemon verbena or mint

(1)   Peel fruit if necessary. Put the flesh in a blender and whizz until smooth, then pass it through a fine sieve to get rid of any pips or fibres. It should now be perfectly smooth.

(2)   Taste it. Add sugar, lemon juice, wine or water to taste. This is also very good if you add herbs such as basil, lemon verbena or mint. You can infuse the herbs in the soup while it is chilling, or add them during the initial blending stage.

(3)   Serve in lovely soup plates or well-chilled glass dishes.

BAKED APPLE
STUFFED WITH MARZIPAN

Nothing accompanies the flavour of baked apple quite like marzipan. You can freeze any leftover marzipan; it will sit happily for up to a year in the freezer, if wrapped properly. However, one chap's marzipan is another chap's poison (after all, cyanide is supposed to taste like bitter almonds; just ask James Bond), so if you are almond-averse, there are equally delicious alternatives: try mincemeat, stem ginger in syrup, raisins with chopped chocolate, or crumbled-up fruit cake soaked in brandy.

◆ INGREDIENTS ◆

Serves 1 – multiply at will

1 Bramley apple, or a large
   eating apple, if you like –
   Bramley is just
   traditional
approx. 75g marzipan
2 tablespoons cider,
brandy, elderflower cordial
   or ginger wine
a few slivered almonds, to
   decorate (optional)
ice cream, cream or Custard
   (page 165), to serve

① Preheat oven to 180°C/gas mark 4.

② Core the apple using a corer or jolly sharp knife (keeping the apple on the board and your wits about you). Slit the skin around the circumference – this will allow the apple to swell nicely and not split. Now stuff the apple by filling its core with marzipan or your chosen filling.

③ Arrange the apple in a baking dish. Bake in the oven for 25–30 minutes or until the apple is soft when pierced with a knife. Serve with your chosen liquor poured over the apple, a scattering of almonds if you are fond of them, and ice cream, cream, Custard or anything else you like.

However much time and effort you spend on creating the puddings in this chapter, please don't go and spoil them all by serving them with lukewarm, lumpy custard or scoops of cheap ice cream. It is really worth spending nearly as much time on the pudding sauce as on the pudding itself. We may even go as far as to say that you can mask a mediocre pudding with a superlative sauce but not the other way round.

CHOCOLATE SAUCE 1

The idea is that you should be able to knock up a chocolate sauce in the blink of an eye. We chaps are not obsessed with chocolate, but it is a useful flavouring and appeals greatly to many ladies, which is reason enough to have a sauce like this under one's belt. Here we give two recipes for chocolate sauce. One can be made with just two ingredients – cream and chocolate – and could not be easier. The other is made with cocoa powder, which we all tend to have lurking at the back of a cupboard (note that it's cocoa and not drinking chocolate: cocoa makes a glossy sauce that tastes superb).

◆ INGREDIENTS ◆

Serves 2–4

150ml cream – single,
   whipping or double
150g dark chocolate
pinch of salt (optional)
slug of brandy, Poire William,
   whisky, rum or whatever
   booze you like

(1) Put the cream and chocolate in a saucepan over a gentle heat and stir while it all melts. That's it! You can add a pinch of salt, to give it a modern touch (if you must). At this point you could also add a slug of whatever booze you like.

(2) Serve the sauce hot, warm or cold. Keep it in the fridge and reheat as needed. It will last for up to 3 days in the fridge.

CHOCOLATE SAUCE 2

◆ INGREDIENTS ◆

Serves 6

500ml single cream
100g sugar – any sort will
   do, but soft brown sugar
   gives a good flavour
100g cocoa
¼ teaspoon salt

(1) Put all the ingredients into a large saucepan, stir over a medium heat, bring to a bubbling simmer and cook, stirring all the time, for 10 minutes until thick and glossy, then serve.

BUTTERSCOTCH SAUCE

This butterscotch sauce is a perfect combination of caramel and cream, entering the realm of the truly sublime. For a cheat's version, simply melt 8–10 butterscotch sweets, such as Wether's Originals, with 100ml cream over a low heat – hey presto.

♦ INGREDIENTS ♦

Serves 4

50g butter
2 tablespoons golden
    syrup
100g sugar – any sort is
    fine
300ml double cream
pinch of salt

(1) Put the butter, syrup and sugar in a saucepan to melt over a gentle heat, stirring frequently.

(2) Now turn up the heat and let the sauce bubble away until it becomes a lovely dark burnished caramel colour – it should smell lovely too. Don't let it catch and burn.

(3) Turn off the heat. Add the cream and salt. Stir to mix. Serve hot or cold.

CUSTARD

It is worth making your own custard. The more you make it, the easier it gets. You can increase the richness of the custard simply by adding more egg yolks. Custard has many uses and there will be very few chaps or chapettes at your table who don't like it.

♦ INGREDIENTS ♦

Serves 4–6

575ml full-fat milk – or
    mixture of milk and cream
    if you like richer custard
1 vanilla pod, split, or
    1 teaspoon vanilla extract
4 egg yolks
1 teaspoon cornflour
50g sugar – caster is best, but
    any type you have handy
    will do

(1) Put the milk and the vanilla pod (if using) in a saucepan and slowly heat almost to the boil. The slow heating will allow the vanilla to infuse the milk with its aroma. If you want it very vanillary, scrape the seeds from the pod directly into the milk.

(2) Mix the egg yolks, cornflour, sugar and vanilla extract (if using) in a medium bowl until they are well combined.

(3) Pour the milk onto the egg mixture (discarding the vanilla pod, if used), whisk or stir thoroughly to combine, and then tip it back into the saucepan. Don't use a non-stick saucepan for this. Over a gentle heat, whisk or stir constantly until it starts to thicken. Keep the mixture moving so that no single spot overheats. Once it has thickened, keep whisking it over the heat for a little longer to ensure the cornflour is fully cooked out.

(4) There is also the option of cooking this more gently in a bain-marie – a bowl suspended over a saucepan of simmering water. It is certainly a great way to keep it warm.

ANGELS ON HORSEBACK

In *Dr. No*, James Bond is offered a lavish dinner by his eponymous nemesis. After a main course of lamb cutlets, Bond chooses, instead of pudding, Angels on Horseback as a savoury, reflecting the Ian Fleming's own lack of a sweet tooth. The dish itself is far more ancient than *Dr. No* and dates back to at least the eighteenth century. There is an American equivalent called Pigs in Blankets, which doesn't have quite the same ring to it.

◆ INGREDIENTS ◆

Serves 4

6 very thin slices of smoked
    streaky bacon
12 shucked oysters, smoked
    oysters or (breaking the
    rules) smoked mussels
Tabasco sauce, lemon wedges
    and toast, to serve
    (optional)

① Stretch the bacon rashers with the back of a knife. Cut in half and wrap each oyster in a slice of bacon. Skewer with a cocktail stick.

② Arrange on a grill pan and grill for 4–5 minutes on each side until the bacon is golden. Serve sizzling hot, on toast if desired. A shake of Tabasco and a squeeze of lemon is a welcome addition.

You could also make this dish with smoked oysters or mussels, which are easily available in cans and should have a home in your larder/store cupboard.

DEVILS ON HORSEBACK

In about 1066, when the Normans were running rampant over the southwest of this fair isle, the soldiers, to make their appearance more grotesque and terrifying, would cover their armour with strips of bacon, and came to be known as 'Devils on Horseback'. Apparently, they would cook the bacon at the end of a busy day terrorising the Cornish. When the dish first made its appearance during the Victorian period, the prunes were stuffed with chutney.

◆ INGREDIENTS ◆

Serves 4

1 Earl Grey teabag
2 tablespoons whisky/ brandy
    (optional)
12 pitted prunes
6 very thin slices of streaky
    bacon

① Put the Earl Grey tea bag in a bowl and pour on 200ml boiling water. Allow to steep for 5 minutes, and then discard the tea bag. Add the booze, if being used, and the prunes. Allow to steep for 30 minutes or overnight.

② Preheat the grill or the oven to 200°C/gas mark 6.

③ Stretch the bacon with the back of a knife. Cut in half and wrap each piece around a prune. Secure with a cocktail stick. Grill for 4–5 minutes on either side or bake in the oven for 8–10 minutes. Remove the cocktail stick and serve.

LOCKETS SAVOURY

✕

This savoury is named after the restaurant where it was created, Lockets, once one of the great London restaurants, along with the Savoy Hotel, Rules and Simpsons-in-the-Strand. It could be accused of being a rather grand version of cheese on toast; however, the use of Stilton rather than a hard Cheddar-type cheese, and especially the addition of a pear, immediately promotes this dish into the category of a gentleman's savoury. Enjoy with a glass of vintage port.

◆ INGREDIENTS ◆

Serves 4

4 slices good-quality white
    bread
50g butter
1 very ripe pear, peeled
    and sliced
200g Stilton, sliced or
    crumbled

① Lightly toast the bread on both sides and butter it generously.

② Preheat the grill or the oven to 200°C/gas mark 6.

③ Arrange the toast on the grill pan (or on a baking sheet if using the oven) and top with a slice of pear and Stilton.

④ Grill gently until bubbling – or bake in the hot oven for 5–7 minutes. Serve on hot plates immediately.

Note: Like English Rabbit (page 139), this recipe is ideal for using up the dregs of the Christmas Stilton (which freezes perfectly, by the way), so you can enjoy it any time. These little toasts have been known to warm the cockles when rustled up for Elevenses or even High Tea.

SCOTCH WOODCOCK

✕

This is Colonel Kenney-Herbert's recipe for a classic English savoury, which used to hold pride of place at both Oxford and Cambridge dining halls, as well as remaining on the House of Commons menu until as late as 1949. The cheat's way of making it is to use Gentlemen's Relish instead of anchovy fillets, but if you used it all up, what would you spread on your toast in the morning? Besides, you may start investigating the recipe for Gentlemen's Relish, which has remained a closely guarded secret since its creation in 1828 by John Osborn, and we would like to keep it that way.

♦ INGREDIENTS ♦

Serves 4

1 tablespoon butter, plus extra
   for the toast
1 can anchovy fillets,
   drained and finely chopped
4 egg yolks
4 slices good white bread

(1) Melt the butter in a bowl suspended over a saucepan of simmering water. Add the anchovies and egg yolks and stir well, until thickened like custard – approx. 10 minutes.

(2) Meanwhile, make the toast and butter it well. Cut the crusts off and cut into quartered triangles. Keep it hot until needed.

(3) Pour the mixture over the slices of hot buttered toast on hot plates, and serve immediately.

AFTER-DINNER EATING

Once every last guest has finished eating the main course, clear away the plates as swiftly as possible (the more polite of your guests will help you do this), and bring to the table the following items: cheese and biscuits, puddings and/or savouries, fruit, port/brandy, chocolates. Then allow your guests to help themselves to whatever they want, in any order. Some like to eat cheese before pudding so they can finish a glass of red wine from main course, while others like to mix it up. With this method, guests can eat as much or as little as they want and no one is under any pressure. The table looks lovely when laden with attractive things, all the guests – and, crucially, the host/ess – can relax and the conversation can flow, rather than being constantly interrupted by someone clearing plates.

INDEX

ACKNOWLEDGEMENTS

CLARE

Thanks to my mother, who never made me clear up the kitchen, so cooking was always fun. Early influences and sublime cooks; Elisabeth Woodhouse, Mary Broadbridge and Odette Duran. The Late Dinah and Christopher Bridge and family, who nurtured my nascent cooking career and were vital inspiration for this book. Special thanks to those who helped me with this book; Janet Dennis who created a mini writer's retreat and talked food with me and generally bucked me up. Jane and Chris Healey (Ultimate Chap), for sharing their country knowledge and recipes on pages 52 and 67 and settling the controversial Bullshot debate. Jumbo the farmer for the sensational kidney recipe on page 105, Fee Sweeney – inspiring cook, Denise Bagnal Oakeley for her wondrous family recipes on pages 68 and 83, Mari Simpson for the first shoot in her beautiful kitchen and legendary recipe on page 121, Kate Simon – all the inspiring Chaps lunches for vital research, Mariana Asprey Newton – great advice, Kai and Martin Henslow at Durleighmarsh and Carolyn and Barry Ballard for the venison; Allyxa Ruby for your incredible kindness and support. Thanks to all those who came along to my Pop-Up home kitchen! The Rogate lady whose family recipe inspired Slivers of Liver on page 143. The lovely people of Harting who were so excited about this book – if you are ever lucky enough to write a recipe book, an unexpected but fantastic part of it is other peoples' enthusiasm to talk about food with you. Working on this project, I had fascinating chats with many people about food and recipes, gardening and game, entertaining and etiquette - I hope I have done it all justice My thanks and appreciation to all at Kyle Books who worked on this book, and to Gustav, my co-author, for believing in this project and for his phenomenal writing talent. Finally, thank you Peeve.

GUSTAV

Thanks to our agent Charlie Viney for making this book happen and to our editor Tara O'Sullivan for bringing it to life.